Shutdown Survival

Shutdown Survival

Matthew Petchinsky

1

Shutdown Survival: A Citizen's Guide to Thriving When Government Stops
By: Matthew Petchinsky

Disclaimer

This book, *Shutdown Survival: A Citizen's Guide to Thriving When Government Stops*, is provided as an informational and educational resource only. It is intended to share general strategies for resilience, preparedness, and personal empowerment during periods of federal government shutdowns, administrative disruptions, or other service interruptions.

The material within does **not** constitute legal, financial, or medical advice. The author is not an attorney, financial advisor, medical professional, or licensed expert in government benefits administration. This work should not be relied upon as a substitute for professional guidance in any of these areas.

This book is **not affiliated with, endorsed by, or sponsored by the United States government, the Social Security Administration, the U.S. Department of Agriculture, or any other federal, state, or local agency.** All references to programs such as Social Security, SSI, SNAP (food stamps), or related benefits are provided for general context only. Readers are strongly encouraged to verify time-sensitive details, eligibility requirements, and program changes directly through official government websites or agencies, as policies and procedures may change frequently and without notice.

The author and publisher make no guarantees regarding the accuracy, completeness, or applicability of the strategies discussed. Readers assume full responsibility for how they apply the information contained herein to their personal circumstances. Any reliance on the material is strictly at the reader's own discretion and risk.

By reading this book, you acknowledge and agree that neither the author nor the publisher can be held liable for any decisions, outcomes, or consequences arising from the use or misuse of the information provided. For urgent questions regarding your benefits, financial situation, or health, consult directly with qualified professionals and official government representatives.

This book is meant to inspire proactive thinking, encourage practical preparation, and promote resourcefulness during uncertain times. Use the insights offered here as tools for building personal resilience—not as a replacement for authoritative sources or professional advice.

Introduction

Government shutdowns are no longer rare, once-in-a-generation anomalies. In recent decades, they have emerged as recurring disruptions—moments where political gridlock halts the machinery of everyday governance. A shutdown occurs when lawmakers fail to pass a budget or funding resolution on time, leaving federal agencies without the legal authority to operate at full capacity. While this may sound like a distant battle in the halls of Congress, its consequences land squarely in the lives of ordinary citizens.

When the government stops, life does not pause. Yet, countless systems that many people rely on—direct deposits for Social Security, timely food stamp approvals, passport processing, tax refunds, student aid, housing assistance, veterans' benefits—are stalled, slowed, or completely frozen. Families waiting on medical authorizations may find their treatments delayed. Parents planning travel may encounter unexpected roadblocks at airports and passport offices. Small businesses counting on federal contracts may suddenly find their income evaporating. These disruptions extend far beyond politics; they ripple through kitchens, workplaces, schools, and hospitals.

The hidden costs of shutdowns are often overlooked. It isn't only about missed paychecks for federal workers. It is about delayed paperwork that stalls a job offer. It is about a medical claim waiting in limbo. It is about the stress of wondering if food assistance will arrive before the pantry is empty. These moments expose the fragility of systems we assume will always run. And yet, they also reveal an overlooked truth: when the "safety net" frays, we are given an opportunity—sometimes an unwelcome one—to weave our own threads of resilience.

This book is not about politics. It does not debate who is right or wrong in Washington, nor does it argue ideology. Instead, it is about **you**. It is about reframing shutdowns as moments where you can step into greater autonomy and stability. Rather than being paralyzed by uncertainty, you can use these times to strengthen your financial resilience, create backup plans for daily needs, build supportive community networks, and foster psychological calm in the face of chaos.

You are not simply a bystander to government dysfunction. You are not at the mercy of gridlock. You are, in fact, the architect of your own stability. With practical tools, creative strategies, and a shift in perspective, you can turn a shutdown from a moment of helplessness into a training ground for preparedness.

This book will guide you through that process. In the chapters ahead, you'll discover how to safeguard your household finances, stretch resources when programs stall, cultivate community-based support systems, and develop the mindset to thrive when uncertainty strikes. Each page is designed to equip you with not just coping skills, but empowering practices that transform shutdown stress into self-reliance and strength.

A government shutdown may close doors—but it can also open new ones. By the end of this book, you will see shutdowns not as roadblocks, but as invitations to grow more resourceful, independent, and prepared for whatever challenges the future may bring.

Chapter 1: The Anatomy of a Shutdown

To understand how to survive and even thrive during a government shutdown, you must first understand what a shutdown actually is—and what it isn't. Popular headlines often reduce shutdowns to political theater, but for everyday people, they represent a very real and immediate disruption in the systems we depend on. This chapter pulls back the curtain to show how shutdowns function, why they happen, and how they filter into the daily lives of citizens.

What a Government Shutdown Actually Means

A government shutdown occurs when Congress fails to pass appropriations legislation—or the President fails to sign it into law—by the beginning of the new fiscal year (October 1) or by the expiration of temporary funding known as a "continuing resolution." Without funding authority, federal agencies cannot continue all of their operations.

However, a shutdown does not mean the entire government ceases to exist overnight. Instead, it forces agencies to divide their activities into two categories:

1. **Essential services** – Operations deemed necessary for the protection of life, property, or national security. These continue to function, though employees may work without immediate pay.
2. **Non-essential services** – Programs or administrative functions not directly tied to urgent safety or security. These are paused, delayed, or shut down entirely until funding is restored.

This distinction is often misunderstood, leading to confusion about why some services continue while others stop. For the public, the challenge lies in knowing which lifelines will still flow and which will temporarily dry up.

Essential vs. Non-Essential Services

Essential services typically include:

- Air traffic control and airport security
- Border protection and national defense
- Law enforcement, including the FBI and federal prisons
- Emergency medical care in federally run facilities
- Power grid and nuclear facility maintenance
- Certain disaster relief operations

These continue to operate, though sometimes with reduced staffing or delayed paychecks for the workers providing them.

Non-essential services often include:

- National parks, museums, and federal cultural sites
- Passport and visa processing (except in urgent cases)
- Most federal research labs and grant administration
- New federal contracts, grants, and loans
- Many administrative offices within federal agencies

The line between "essential" and "non-essential" is not about importance in daily life—it is about whether a function is considered immediately critical to safety. That means many programs that households rely on for stability, though vital, fall into the category of delayed or disrupted.

How Shutdowns Impact Benefits

For millions of Americans, the first question in a shutdown is: *What happens to my benefits?* The answer depends on how each program is funded and whether it has reserve money outside the annual appropriations cycle.

Social Security & SSI (Supplemental Security Income)

- **Social Security (retirement and disability benefits):** These payments generally continue during shutdowns because they are funded through a permanent trust fund, not the yearly budget.
- **SSI (Supplemental Security Income):** More vulnerable. While benefits may continue for a short time, administrative functions like new applications, appeals, or changes to existing cases may stall. If the shutdown extends, future payments can become uncertain.

SNAP (Supplemental Nutrition Assistance Program, or "food stamps")

- SNAP benefits are federally funded but distributed monthly through state systems. During a shutdown, the USDA may use contingency funds to keep payments going temporarily. However, if the shutdown drags on, states may run out of money to issue benefits, leaving families in limbo. Application processing and renewals are often delayed.

Medicare & Medicaid

- These programs typically continue because they are funded by trust funds and mandatory spending, not annual appropriations.
- That said, customer service hotlines, claims processing, and new provider approvals may face slowdowns. Delays in medical authorizations or billing resolutions are common.

Other Benefits and Services

- **Unemployment insurance:** Largely funded at the state level, but federal oversight and supplemental funds may be delayed.
- **Veterans' benefits:** Core benefits usually continue, but new claims or appeals may be slowed.
- **Housing assistance (HUD vouchers, Section 8):** Payments can be interrupted, leaving tenants and landlords uncertain.

The Domino Effect of Delays

Even if your check still arrives, the *administrative machinery* often grinds to a halt. This can include:

- **Paperwork bottlenecks:** New applications for benefits sit idle.
- **Medical delays:** Prior authorizations for treatments or prescriptions get stuck in review.
- **Travel issues:** Passports and visas may be delayed for weeks or months.
- **Business disruptions:** Federal loans, contracts, and grants can be frozen mid-process.

Shutdowns reveal how interconnected these systems are. A delayed signature on a form in one office can cascade into weeks of uncertainty for a family or business waiting on approval.

Reframing the Shutdown

At first glance, shutdowns are frightening—especially for those living paycheck-to-paycheck or depending on federal programs. But there is another way to see them: as **wake-up calls**. They expose just how dependent society has become on centralized systems, and they remind us of the need to cultivate resilience outside of them.

When you know which services are vulnerable, you can plan accordingly. You can build buffers, create personal workarounds, and develop community support systems that shield you from the full force of disruption. Shutdowns are not just moments of crisis; they are opportunities to learn, adapt, and take greater ownership of your future stability.

Key Takeaways from Chapter 1

- A government shutdown happens when Congress fails to approve funding.
- "Essential" services (safety, security, defense) continue, while "non-essential" ones pause.
- Social Security usually continues, but SSI, SNAP, housing aid, and administrative processes are vulnerable to delay or disruption.
- Medicare and Medicaid payments continue, but authorizations and paperwork may be slowed.
- Shutdowns create ripple effects that impact households, businesses, and communities.
- With awareness and preparation, you can turn shutdown uncertainty into a chance to build autonomy and resilience.

Chapter 2: The Money Pause — Protecting Income & Benefits

When a government shutdown strikes, money becomes the most immediate concern. Not just the paycheck, but the invisible streams of income and support that keep households steady: SSI deposits, SNAP recertifications, tax refunds, and unemployment filings. For millions of families, these are lifelines, and any delay in their delivery feels like the ground shifting beneath their feet.

This chapter provides a clear-eyed look at how shutdowns interrupt financial flows—and, most importantly, how you can protect yourself. Think of it as designing your own shock absorber: strategies to cushion against the sudden pause, and habits that transform crisis into preparedness.

Understanding the "Money Pause"

A government shutdown doesn't necessarily stop benefits outright, but it *does* slow or suspend the processes that keep them consistent. Payments may be delayed. New applications can stall. Backlogs build. And refunds or recertifications may get pushed further and further down the line.

The money pause shows up in four major areas:

1. **SSI (Supplemental Security Income):** Monthly payments may continue briefly, but shutdowns strain the administrative systems. New claims, appeals, or adjustments often freeze in place. Extended shutdowns raise uncertainty about continued disbursement.
2. **SNAP (food stamps):** Benefits may flow temporarily using contingency funds, but a prolonged shutdown can drain reserves. Recertifications and new applications are typically delayed, leaving families with shrinking balances and no clear timeline for replenishment.

3.Tax refunds: During shutdowns, the IRS scales back operations. Refunds may be delayed, audits paused, and processing times stretched far beyond normal. For households depending on refunds for large purchases or debt relief, this becomes a major stress point.

4.Unemployment filings: While unemployment insurance is state-administered, federal oversight and supplemental funds can be disrupted. Shutdowns often create processing delays and reduce customer service availability, slowing access to critical support.

Preparing for Delays

The key to surviving a shutdown is not panic, but preparation. While you cannot control government timelines, you can create financial breathing room and systems of your own.

1. Build a Buffer — Even Small One Counts

- **Emergency stash:** Even $100–$200 saved in cash or a separate account can bridge small gaps in groceries or utilities.
- **Food storage:** Keep at least 1–2 weeks' worth of shelf-stable meals (rice, beans, pasta, canned vegetables, peanut butter) to reduce dependence on immediate benefit replenishment.
- **Medication supply:** Work with your doctor or pharmacy to have a cushion of necessary prescriptions, if possible.

2. Accelerate Applications Before Deadlines

- Submit SNAP recertifications or SSI paperwork *early* whenever possible. A backlog is less likely to affect you if your paperwork is already in the system.
- File taxes as soon as you are eligible; don't wait for the April rush, when shutdown delays may hit hardest.
- Refile unemployment paperwork or updates promptly, even if the system feels slow. The sooner your file is in the queue, the better.

3. Diversify Income Streams

Shutdowns highlight the danger of single points of failure. Consider:

- **Gig work or freelancing:** Even temporary side income (delivery apps, online services, tutoring, odd jobs) creates independence from government timelines.
- **Community barter:** Trading skills, childcare, or goods locally reduces reliance on cash flow alone.
- **Part-time opportunities:** Seasonal or short-term work, especially around the holidays, can create extra cushioning.

4. Cut Unnecessary Outflow

- Review subscriptions, memberships, and recurring expenses. Pausing non-essentials during shutdown uncertainty can stretch what you already have.
- Shift grocery spending toward staples and away from luxury or convenience items.
- Re-negotiate bills if possible: some utility and phone companies allow hardship extensions.

Short-Term Cushioning Strategies

If benefits are delayed, how do you survive the immediate gap?

- **Local food banks and pantries:** Many expand services during shutdowns. Check regional nonprofits or faith-based centers (services are usually open to all, regardless of religious affiliation).
- **Community assistance networks:** Mutual aid groups, local charities, and neighborhood networks can provide meals, cash support, or childcare during crises.
- **Credit wisely:** If you must borrow, prioritize low- or no-interest options (credit union loans, family loans) over high-interest payday lenders.
- **Cash conservation tactics:** Limit ATM withdrawals and carry only what you need day-to-day. This prevents impulse spending and stretches reserves.

Psychological Anchors in a Money Pause

Financial stress is not just logistical—it is deeply emotional. Shutdowns create uncertainty, and uncertainty breeds anxiety. Protecting your mindset is as vital as protecting your wallet.

- **Reframe the pause:** Instead of viewing delayed payments as disaster, see them as prompts to test your resourcefulness.
- **Track what you *do* control:** Food inventory, bill priorities, transportation costs, and community contacts.
- **Create "micro-goals":** Each day, focus on one action that increases your resilience—a phone call, a meal prep, a neighborly exchange. Small wins reduce the feeling of helplessness.

Looking Ahead

The money pause is temporary—but the lessons it teaches can last a lifetime. Every shutdown is a reminder of how fragile centralized systems are. By creating buffers, diversifying income, and cultivating a community safety net, you transform shutdowns from episodes of chaos into catalysts for personal stability.

Key Takeaways from Chapter 2

- Shutdowns delay SSI processing, SNAP recertifications, tax refunds, and unemployment filings.
- Build small financial and food buffers to cushion against uncertainty.
- File paperwork early and diversify income streams before a shutdown occurs.
- Use local networks and nonprofits to bridge short-term gaps.
- Psychological resilience—anchoring your mindset—is as crucial as financial preparation.

Chapter 3: Food Security Beyond SNAP

When a government shutdown hits, one of the first and most personal worries is food. For households relying on SNAP, the uncertainty is immediate: Will benefits load on time? Will recertification be delayed? Will contingency funds run out? Even for those not on assistance, the fear of grocery costs rising or shelves thinning during prolonged disruptions adds pressure.

Food is more than calories. It is security, stability, and dignity. When the official systems wobble, the best safeguard is to take ownership of your food supply with practical, creative, and community-driven strategies. This chapter will show you how to design a food safety net that goes beyond SNAP—so you can eat well, share generously, and stay steady through the turbulence of a shutdown.

The Reality of Food Delays

While SNAP benefits may continue temporarily, extended shutdowns can exhaust reserves. Application processing slows. Recertifications may sit in backlog. Meanwhile, food pantries and nonprofits see spikes in demand, creating longer lines and limited supplies. Even if you're not directly affected by SNAP, grocery chains may feel the ripple effects, from delayed USDA programs to interrupted food inspection services.

That means food insecurity can spread wider than expected, touching households across income levels. Preparation now is the key to stability later.

Pantry Planning as a Survival Skill

A resilient household starts with a **thoughtful pantry.** This is not about panic buying—it's about steady, intentional preparation.

1. Build a Core Reserve

Stock foods with long shelf lives that form the backbone of meals:

- **Grains:** rice, oats, pasta, quinoa, flour.
- **Legumes:** dried beans, lentils, chickpeas.
- **Proteins:** canned tuna, chicken, peanut butter, powdered eggs, shelf-stable tofu.
- **Vegetables:** canned tomatoes, corn, peas, green beans.
- **Fats & oils:** olive oil, coconut oil, shelf-stable butter substitutes.
- **Flavor essentials:** salt, sugar, bouillon cubes, spices.

A two- to four-week supply can dramatically reduce stress during benefit delays.

2. Rotate, Don't Hoard

The best pantry is one you use daily. Create a rotation system where the oldest items are eaten first. Replace them on your next trip. This keeps food fresh and prevents waste.

3. Plan Around Meals, Not Items

Instead of stocking random goods, think in terms of meal kits:

- Rice + beans + canned salsa = burrito bowls.
- Pasta + canned tomatoes + dried herbs = simple marinara.
- Oats + powdered milk + peanut butter = protein-rich breakfast.

When your pantry is built on complete meals, stress is reduced because you don't have to improvise under pressure.

The Power of Bulk Buying

Bulk buying is one of the most cost-effective ways to stretch dollars and create stability.

- **Warehouse clubs and co-ops:** Pool memberships with friends or family if costs feel high. Buying in bulk reduces per-unit cost and ensures a longer-lasting reserve.
- **Staple foods in 25–50 lb bags:** Rice, beans, flour, oats—these can last months if stored in airtight containers.
- **Seasonal preservation:** Buy fruits or vegetables in season (often cheapest) and freeze, can, or dehydrate them.
- **Shared freezers:** If you lack space, consider splitting bulk purchases with a neighbor who has storage capacity.

Bulk buying is not only about saving money—it reduces the frequency of shopping trips, which matters during uncertain times when benefits, fuel, or supply chains may be strained.

Neighborhood Food-Sharing Circles

No household should shoulder food insecurity alone. One of the most powerful responses to shutdowns is **collective resilience.**

1. Create a Food Circle

- Gather neighbors, friends, or extended family to form a local sharing group.
- Each member commits to contributing in small ways—whether food, skills, or time.
- Build a rotating meal schedule where households take turns hosting or preparing shared meals.

2. Swap & Share Systems

- **Skill swaps:** One neighbor bakes bread, another cans vegetables, another cooks soups.
- **Ingredient swaps:** Trade what you have in surplus for what you lack.
- **Freezers & gardens:** A neighbor with freezer space can store bulk meat for several families; gardeners can share seasonal produce.

3. Emergency Meal Network

Set up a simple phone tree or messaging group. If a household runs out of food mid-month or during a benefit delay, the group can respond quickly with a shared meal or grocery pickup.

Low-Cost Food Strategies

Shutdown resilience doesn't mean spending more. It means spending smarter:

- **Batch cooking:** Make large portions of soups, stews, and casseroles that can stretch for multiple meals.
- **Meat as flavor, not centerpiece:** Use smaller portions of meat with beans, grains, or vegetables to create filling meals.
- **DIY snacks:** Popcorn kernels, homemade granola, or baked goods cost far less than packaged snacks.
- **Tap hidden resources:** Many community centers, churches, and even libraries host pop-up food distributions during shutdowns.

The Emotional Side of Food Security

Food is deeply tied to peace of mind. An empty fridge magnifies stress. A stocked pantry—even a modest one—provides psychological safety. Knowing you have meals ready allows you to approach shutdowns with calm instead of panic.

Creating food-sharing networks also combats the isolation that often accompanies economic stress. Eating together, even in hard times, reinforces community bonds and restores dignity where scarcity tries to sow shame.

Looking Ahead

Food security is the foundation of shutdown survival. With a well-planned pantry, smart bulk buying, and supportive neighborhood food-sharing circles, you can ensure that your household never goes hungry—even when offices slow down and benefits are delayed.

Key Takeaways from Chapter 3

- SNAP benefits can stall; pantry planning ensures independence.
- Build a rotating reserve of staple foods for 2–4 weeks.
- Bulk buying and seasonal preservation stretch dollars and reduce vulnerability.
- Food-sharing circles create community-based safety nets.
- A stocked pantry provides both physical nourishment and emotional stability.

Chapter 4: Healthcare in Limbo

When the federal government shuts down, the impact on healthcare is often invisible at first. Hospitals don't close their doors overnight, and prescriptions don't immediately vanish from pharmacy shelves. But beneath the surface, cracks begin to spread—claims stall, approvals freeze, and overburdened systems slow to a crawl. For those relying on veterans' care, Medicare paperwork, or FDA-reviewed medications, shutdowns create a ripple effect that can jeopardize both health and peace of mind.

This chapter breaks down how shutdowns affect the healthcare landscape, while offering strategies to safeguard your access to medicine, appointments, and essential care when government functions falter.

The Shutdown Effect on Healthcare

Healthcare in the United States is a complex web of public and private systems. While hospitals remain open and most medical providers continue working, the machinery that supports them is often tied to federal agencies. Shutdowns may not cut off care entirely, but they slow the gears that keep the system running smoothly.

VA Hospitals and Veterans' Health Services

- **Open but strained:** VA medical centers and hospitals typically remain open because they are funded through separate appropriations cycles. However, new claims, appeals, and administrative functions may grind to a halt.
- **Delayed reimbursements:** Veterans may face delays in travel reimbursements, benefit processing, or prescription shipments.
- **Mental health support:** Shutdowns often reduce staffing in crisis hotlines and outreach programs, adding stress to already vulnerable populations.

Medicare and Medicaid

- **Benefits continue:** Payments for Medicare and Medicaid services generally flow, since they are funded through trust funds and mandatory spending.
- **Paperwork stalls:** New applications, provider enrollments, appeals, and claims processing may slow significantly. This can lead to denied services if paperwork isn't approved in time.
- **Customer service lines:** Many hotlines are reduced or closed, making it harder to get answers during shutdown periods.

FDA Approvals and Public Health Oversight

- **Drug and device approvals:** Shutdowns often force the FDA to halt or delay review of new medications, devices, and food safety inspections. This doesn't affect drugs already on shelves, but it can delay access to new treatments.
- **Food and drug safety inspections:** With fewer inspections, risks in the food supply chain may increase. While unlikely to collapse overnight, the slowdown erodes oversight and consumer protection.

Keeping Prescriptions Filled

One of the most immediate concerns during a shutdown is making sure prescriptions remain uninterrupted. Here's how to prepare:

1. Build a Medication Cushion

- Ask your doctor about a **90-day prescription supply** instead of 30 days. Many insurance plans allow this, especially through mail-order services.
- Refill prescriptions **as soon as they are eligible,** not at the last minute.
- If your medication has no generic backup, explore assistance programs from manufacturers or local nonprofits that can provide short-term support.

2. Use Mail Order Wisely

- Mail-order pharmacies often provide longer supplies and lower costs, but they can be vulnerable during shutdowns if shipping delays occur. Keep at least a short supply locally as backup.

3. Keep a List of Alternatives

- Work with your healthcare provider to identify safe backup medications in case shortages occur.
- For common medications (such as antibiotics, pain relievers, or blood pressure drugs), ask about over-the-counter or therapeutic substitutes you can use temporarily if access becomes disrupted.

Scheduling Ahead

Shutdowns create backlogs in paperwork-heavy healthcare processes. To reduce your risk:

- **Schedule early:** Book medical appointments, surgeries, or lab work ahead of funding deadlines (September 30 is the key date). If you wait until a shutdown begins, scheduling may freeze.
- **Submit paperwork quickly:** Medicare and Medicaid claims, VA paperwork, or disability medical reviews should be filed as soon as possible to avoid being stuck in the backlog.
- **Keep copies:** Always keep digital and paper copies of submitted documents in case systems lose track of them.

Backup Systems for Healthcare Stability

Sometimes the best protection is redundancy. By creating multiple access points to care, you reduce the chance of being stranded.

1. Community Health Clinics

- Federally Qualified Health Centers (FQHCs) often continue operating even during shutdowns, as they receive separate funding. They provide sliding-scale primary care, dental, and mental health services.
- Many urban and rural areas also have nonprofit clinics that can serve as backups if paperwork stalls elsewhere.

2. Pharmacy Programs

- Large pharmacy chains often run their own discount programs, offering lower-cost generics even without insurance.
- Some also provide temporary emergency supplies for patients caught in benefit delays.

3. Telehealth Options

- Many insurance plans and independent platforms provide low-cost telehealth visits.
- These services can help with prescription refills, mental health support, or urgent questions when in-person access is disrupted.

4. Emergency Cash or Card Reserve

- Keep a small reserve ($100–$200 if possible) specifically for medical costs in case insurance reimbursement or benefit payments are delayed.

Protecting Mental Health in Shutdown Times

Shutdowns affect more than physical health—they create uncertainty that strains mental wellbeing. Anxiety about losing care, running out of medication, or being denied coverage can spiral quickly.

Practical steps:

- **Create a self-care toolkit:** Include relaxation exercises, journaling, or grounding techniques to manage stress.
- **Stay connected:** Reach out to community groups, veterans' networks, or local mental health resources for support.
- **Use free hotlines:** Crisis lines remain active even during shutdowns. Keep a list of numbers handy for yourself or loved ones.

Looking Ahead

Healthcare may not disappear during a shutdown, but the delays, disruptions, and uncertainty can feel just as dangerous. By scheduling ahead, keeping prescriptions filled, and building multiple safety nets, you can stay anchored in stability even while paperwork and approvals sit in limbo.

Key Takeaways from Chapter 4

- VA hospitals remain open but face administrative delays.
- Medicare/Medicaid payments continue, but paperwork and claims may freeze.
- FDA approvals and inspections slow, impacting future treatments and food oversight.
- Protect your prescriptions with 90-day supplies, early refills, and backups.
- Schedule appointments and paperwork before shutdown deadlines.
- Build redundancy with clinics, pharmacies, telehealth, and small emergency cash reserves.
- Mental health care is just as critical as physical care during times of disruption.

Chapter 5: Children & Families in Flux

Government shutdowns don't just create ripples for individuals—they shake entire households. Nowhere is this more visible than in families with young children. For parents, caregivers, and guardians, the stress of delayed benefits or paused services is compounded by the urgent need to keep children nourished, safe, and stable.

Programs designed to support children—such as Head Start, school meal initiatives, and WIC (Women, Infants, and Children)—become vulnerable during shutdowns. When these safety nets falter, families are left to improvise solutions. The good news: with preparation, awareness, and creative stopgaps, parents can keep their families steady even when government systems grind to a halt.

Head Start and Early Education Disruptions

Head Start programs, which provide early education, meals, and support for low-income families, rely heavily on federal funding. During a shutdown:

- **New funding freezes:** Local programs may not receive their grants on time, forcing temporary closures or reduced services.
- **Staff furloughs:** Teachers, aides, and administrators may be sent home without pay, leaving classrooms understaffed or closed.
- **Ripple effect:** Parents relying on Head Start for childcare may suddenly need backup arrangements to continue working.

Preparation tips for parents:

1. **Identify alternative childcare early.** Reach out to family, friends, or trusted neighbors who could provide temporary care if your program closes.
2. **Network with other Head Start parents.** Shared babysitting rotations or group care arrangements can fill the gap.
3. **Ask about emergency funds.** Some states or local nonprofits provide stopgap grants for childcare in times of disruption.

School Meal Programs

For many children, breakfast and lunch at school are more than routine—they are essential. Federal funding supports free and reduced-price meals through the National School Lunch Program and School Breakfast Program. During a shutdown:

- **Short-term continuation:** Schools may use carryover funds for a time, but prolonged shutdowns can deplete resources.
- **Meal reductions:** Some districts may scale back offerings or limit who qualifies if funding uncertainty continues.
- **Summer meals and after-school snacks:** These programs may be paused if appropriations are delayed.

Stopgap tools for parents:

- **Stock simple lunch staples:** Peanut butter, tuna, crackers, applesauce cups, granola bars, and shelf-stable milk can create quick replacements for school meals.
- **Batch cook & freeze:** Prepare large batches of kid-friendly meals (pasta, soups, casseroles) and portion them into freezer containers.
- **Coordinate parent meal co-ops:** Families can rotate preparing group meals for multiple children, reducing the burden on any single household.

WIC (Women, Infants, and Children)

WIC provides targeted nutritional support for pregnant women, infants, and young children. Shutdowns disrupt WIC in critical ways:

- **Voucher pauses:** New vouchers may not be issued if federal funds stall.
- **Clinic closures:** WIC clinics may reduce hours, limit staff, or close temporarily.
- **Vendor limitations:** Some grocery stores may stop accepting WIC if reimbursements are delayed.

Protective strategies:

1. **Redeem vouchers immediately.** Don't wait until the end of the month. Stock up early when you can.
2. **Stock essentials outside WIC:** Keep extra formula, baby food, and staple items like cereal, milk, and juice in reserve.
3. **Tap local networks:** Food pantries and mutual aid groups often create baby- and child-specific supply banks during crises.

Building Family Stopgap Systems

Parents can ease the burden of shutdown disruptions by creating layered systems of resilience:

1. Food Reserves for Kids

- Focus on shelf-stable favorites: mac and cheese, oatmeal packets, dried fruit, and snack bars.
- Keep a "child comfort shelf" with a few treats—cookies, hot chocolate, fruit cups—to preserve a sense of normalcy.

2. Emergency Childcare Plans

- Draft a backup schedule with friends, family, or other parents in your area.
- Explore co-op childcare models where parents rotate supervision duties during the day.

3. Community Networks

- Join or create neighborhood parent groups. These circles can share food, supplies, and childcare in emergencies.
- Use schools, libraries, or community centers as hubs to connect with other families facing the same challenges.

4. Financial Preparation

- Set aside a "kid cushion" of \$20–\$50 if possible, dedicated to school lunches, emergency daycare, or supplies.
- Stretch resources by cooking in bulk, shopping co-ops, or buying secondhand clothes and supplies during stable times.

Psychological Stability for Children

Children absorb the stress of their environment. Shutdowns can create fear and confusion if parents appear panicked. To reduce emotional strain:

- **Maintain routines.** Bedtimes, homework schedules, and family meals should remain consistent.
- **Be honest but reassuring.** Explain shutdowns in simple terms: "Some programs are closed right now, but we have what we need and we'll take care of each other."
- **Create a sense of participation.** Let kids help cook, pack lunches, or organize supplies. This empowers them instead of leaving them anxious.
- **Protect play.** Even in crisis, make room for games, storytelling, and fun. Play is resilience for children.

Looking Ahead

Families are at the heart of any shutdown's ripple effects. From Head Start closures to paused WIC vouchers, children and parents feel disruptions quickly. But forethought, community support, and creative stopgaps can turn uncertainty into stability. By preparing ahead, families can ensure that children stay fed, cared for, and emotionally secure—even when federal programs stall.

Key Takeaways from Chapter 5

- Head Start programs may pause, requiring parents to plan backup childcare.
- School meal programs can face delays or reductions; families should prepare lunch alternatives and batch meals.
- WIC vouchers and clinics may be disrupted—redeem benefits early and build small reserves.
- Stopgap systems (food reserves, childcare co-ops, parent networks) build resilience.
- Children need emotional stability through routines, reassurance, and play.

Chapter 6: When Paychecks Freeze

For hundreds of thousands of federal employees and contractors, a government shutdown is not an abstract policy issue—it is an immediate paycheck crisis. In past shutdowns, workers have gone weeks or even months without pay, with only the promise of "back pay" once the stalemate ended. Contractors, unlike federal employees, often don't receive that back pay at all.

This chapter explores the stark reality of frozen paychecks and provides strategies to protect income, diversify revenue streams, and even thrive through alternative financial models such as side hustles and bartering.

The Human Impact of Frozen Paychecks

When a shutdown begins:

- **Federal employees** in "non-essential" roles are furloughed—sent home without pay. Many continue to show up for work in "essential" roles but are not paid until the shutdown ends.
- **Contractors** often face immediate layoffs or unpaid work stoppages. Unlike federal employees, they are rarely guaranteed retroactive pay.
- **Ripple effect:** Missed paychecks affect rent, mortgage, car payments, groceries, childcare, and debt obligations. Financial stress spreads quickly, and many families are forced to dip into savings or credit.

Shutdowns reveal the fragility of relying on a single employer, even one as massive as the federal government. For workers caught in the middle, preparation and creative adaptation are crucial.

Income Diversification: Building Multiple Streams

The most powerful buffer against a frozen paycheck is not a bigger emergency fund alone, but **diversified income sources.** When one stream dries up, others keep flowing.

1. Side Hustles That Scale Quickly

- **Delivery services:** Driving for apps like Uber, Lyft, DoorDash, or Instacart can produce same-week income.
- **Freelancing online:** Writing, graphic design, tutoring, coding, and virtual assistance are in high demand on platforms like Upwork or Fiverr.
- **Seasonal jobs:** Retail, warehouse, or hospitality positions often need immediate hires, especially during holiday seasons.

2. Skills-Based Income

- Identify personal skills (carpentry, childcare, tutoring, cooking) that can be monetized locally.
- Offer lessons in music, fitness, or academics to supplement income.
- Sell crafts or handmade goods through local markets or online platforms.

3. Rental or Asset-Based Income

- Rent out a spare room through short-term platforms.
- Consider car-sharing services or equipment rentals (tools, cameras, etc.).
- Monetize unused assets: extra furniture, appliances, or collectibles can bring fast cash through resale.

Bartering as an Alternative Economy

When money is tight, bartering becomes a lifeline. Exchanging skills, services, or goods eliminates the need for immediate cash while still meeting household needs.

Examples of Shutdown Bartering

- **Childcare for food:** Parents swap babysitting hours in exchange for groceries.
- **Repairs for meals:** Someone handy with home or auto repairs trades work for cooked meals or pantry staples.
- **Skills for services:** A teacher provides tutoring in exchange for haircut services or pet care.

How to Build a Barter Circle

1. **List your skills and assets.** Write down what you can offer and what you most need.
2. **Connect with neighbors.** Community boards, churches, libraries, and local Facebook groups often host barter exchanges.
3. **Create trust systems.** Start with small exchanges to build confidence, then expand to higher-value trades.
4. **Document agreements.** Even casual bartering benefits from clarity—make sure both parties know what's expected.

Bartering does more than cover gaps; it builds community resilience and reduces dependence on fragile monetary systems during shutdowns.

Financial Survival Strategies for Frozen Paychecks
When income is interrupted, timing and discipline matter.

1. Prioritize Essential Expenses

- Focus on housing, utilities, food, and medical needs first.
- Contact lenders early to request hardship deferments or payment plans—many banks adjust terms during shutdowns.

2. Use Resources Wisely

- Tap employee assistance programs or union relief funds.
- Explore nonprofit emergency funds, many of which launch specifically to support workers during shutdowns.
- Food pantries, mutual aid groups, and local charities often step in when paychecks are delayed.

3. Avoid High-Cost Debt Traps

- Payday lenders and predatory loans may appear tempting, but the cycle of debt they create is far more damaging than a temporary disruption.
- If borrowing is unavoidable, seek low-interest options through credit unions or personal networks.

Psychological Shifts: From Victimhood to Agency

The hardest part of a frozen paycheck is not just the missing money—it's the loss of control. Workers feel caught between political battles they did not choose, yet they carry the financial consequences. Reframing this experience as an opportunity for self-empowerment changes the dynamic.

- **Agency mindset:** Ask, "What can I create, sell, or trade today?" rather than "What can't I afford?"
- **Shutdown as a signal:** Use the crisis as motivation to build new income streams that endure beyond the shutdown.
- **Community wealth:** Recognize that resilience is not built alone; it grows in networks of exchange, trust, and cooperation.

Looking Ahead

Frozen paychecks remind us that even the largest employer in the world can falter. For federal employees and contractors, shutdowns highlight the necessity of building personal financial ecosystems beyond a single job. Through diversification, side hustles, bartering, and resilience strategies, a paycheck freeze can shift from a devastating blow to a catalyst for long-term stability.

Key Takeaways from Chapter 6

- Shutdowns create immediate income loss for federal employees and contractors, with contractors least likely to recover lost wages.
- Diversifying income through side hustles, freelancing, and asset-based revenue provides essential cushioning.
- Bartering creates a cash-free safety net and strengthens community ties.
- Prioritize essentials, negotiate with lenders, and avoid predatory debt.
- A shift in mindset—from dependence on one paycheck to self-directed agency—turns crisis into resilience.

Chapter 7: Housing & Stability

Housing is more than shelter—it is the foundation of safety, dignity, and stability. When the government shuts down, disruptions in housing programs like HUD, Section 8, and federal mortgage approvals put that foundation under strain. For millions of renters and homeowners, the uncertainty can feel like an earthquake beneath their feet.

This chapter explores how shutdowns ripple through housing systems, what that means for tenants, landlords, and aspiring homeowners, and—most importantly—how you can prepare fallback strategies to keep a roof over your head.

Housing Programs in Shutdown Times

HUD (U.S. Department of Housing and Urban Development)

During a shutdown, HUD's operations slow dramatically:

- **Administrative paralysis:** Grant applications, renewals, and inspections stall.
- **Housing assistance disruption:** Rental subsidies and vouchers may be delayed if funding expires.
- **Community development programs:** Local housing agencies may suspend progress on community block grants or maintenance projects.

While HUD often uses reserve funds to keep some programs running temporarily, those reserves are not unlimited. A prolonged shutdown quickly depletes them.

Section 8 Housing Choice Vouchers

- **Payments to landlords:** In short shutdowns, landlords may continue to receive subsidy checks, but extended shutdowns can interrupt payments, leaving tenants vulnerable.
- **Landlord uncertainty:** Some landlords, especially smaller ones, may pressure tenants for full rent when subsidy payments stall.
- **Applications and transfers:** New voucher approvals, moves to new housing, and recertifications may freeze in place.

Mortgage Approvals and FHA Loans

- **FHA and USDA loans:** Federal Housing Administration and U.S. Department of Agriculture home loans may face significant delays. Applications sit in backlog until staffing resumes.
- **VA home loans:** Veterans may see delays in processing, even if approvals eventually resume.
- **Ripple effect:** Families planning to purchase or refinance may lose favorable interest rates or deals as timelines collapse.

The Human Cost of Housing Delays

For renters: the threat of eviction looms if landlords refuse to wait for delayed HUD or Section 8 payments. For homeowners: loan approvals stall, refinances are missed, and closing dates fall apart. For those already on the margins, shutdowns can mean choosing between food, medicine, or rent.

Housing stress is one of the most destabilizing effects of shutdowns, because losing shelter creates cascading crises in employment, education, and health. The goal, then, is not just to survive a single missed payment, but to build systems of negotiation and fallback that keep housing secure.

Strategies for Renters

1. Open Communication with Landlords

- **Contact early:** Don't wait until rent is overdue. Let landlords know immediately if Section 8 or HUD payments are delayed.
- **Provide documentation:** Share official notices or letters proving the delay is due to a federal shutdown, not personal negligence.
- **Negotiate partial payments:** Offer to pay your portion of rent (or as much as you can afford) while subsidies are paused. This demonstrates good faith.

2. Leverage Tenant Protections

- **Local laws:** Many cities and states have eviction moratoriums or hardship provisions during government crises. Learn your rights ahead of time.
- **Legal aid:** Local nonprofit legal organizations often assist tenants facing eviction threats during shutdowns.

3. Emergency Rental Aid

- **Nonprofit funds:** Many community organizations, churches, and charities establish emergency rental assistance funds during shutdowns.
- **Local housing authorities:** Even if federal funds pause, local agencies may tap reserves or coordinate with nonprofits to protect vulnerable renters.
- **Mutual aid groups:** Community networks often mobilize rent support for affected families.

Strategies for Homeowners

1. Prepare for Mortgage Delays

- FHA, VA, and USDA mortgage approvals may be stalled. Plan timelines with flexibility if you are buying or refinancing.
- If possible, lock interest rates early to avoid financial loss if closings are delayed.

2. Contact Your Lender Early

- Many lenders offer **forbearance programs** for homeowners directly affected by shutdowns.
- Document your situation (e.g., furlough notices, delayed subsidy paperwork) to strengthen your case.

3. Explore Refinancing Alternatives

- Credit unions or local banks may provide bridging loans or alternative refinancing if federal programs are stuck.

Fallback Housing Planning

Sometimes the best defense is a layered safety net. Consider these fallback strategies:

- **Emergency fund for housing:** Even \$100–\$300 set aside for rent or mortgage can buy critical time.
- **Roommate or co-living options:** If housing costs become unmanageable, sharing space reduces expenses.
- **Family fallback:** Establish agreements with relatives or friends for temporary shelter if eviction or foreclosure becomes unavoidable.
- **Short-term rental aid groups:** Many nonprofits create "housing crisis grants" specifically for families on the brink during shutdowns.

Creative Community Solutions

Housing resilience grows stronger in community.

- **Shared housing networks:** Neighbors may open rooms to furloughed workers or families in need.
- **Barter with landlords:** In small-scale situations, tenants may offer repairs, maintenance, or services in exchange for temporary rent relief.
- **Tenant associations:** Organizing with fellow tenants strengthens negotiating power and provides a support system if landlords apply pressure.

Psychological Stability in Housing Stress

Few stresses weigh heavier than the fear of losing your home. To manage this strain:

- **Focus on agency:** Every phone call, every negotiation, every document submitted is a step toward control.
- **Create a fallback plan in writing:** Knowing exactly where you would go and what steps you'd take if eviction loomed helps reduce panic.
- **Lean on networks:** Talking with other renters or homeowners facing the same crisis reduces isolation and builds solidarity.

Looking Ahead

Housing disruptions during shutdowns expose the fragility of relying solely on government-administered support. By communicating early, negotiating wisely, and building fallback systems, you can secure stability for yourself and your family—even when HUD, Section 8, and mortgage offices stall.

Key Takeaways from Chapter 7

- HUD and Section 8 payments may be delayed, creating stress for renters and landlords.
- Mortgage approvals (FHA, VA, USDA) often stall during shutdowns, impacting buyers and homeowners.
- Renters should communicate early, provide documentation, and explore partial payment or emergency rental aid.
- Homeowners can request forbearance, seek alternative lenders, and plan for closing delays.
- Fallback housing plans and community solutions add resilience during uncertain times.
- Psychological preparation—knowing your next steps—reduces the fear that comes with housing instability.

Chapter 8: Emotional & Mental Resilience

Shutdowns are not only financial or logistical crises—they are psychological ones. When paychecks freeze, benefits stall, or housing support becomes uncertain, stress compounds quickly. Fear of the unknown often weighs heavier than the practical delays themselves. Anxiety spikes, depression deepens, and families find themselves not only struggling with bills but also with sleepless nights, arguments, and an erosion of hope.

This chapter shifts the focus inward: to the emotional survival skills that turn shutdown stress into resilience. By practicing grounding techniques, journaling through uncertainty, and leaning into community connections, you can safeguard your mental health while building a mindset that thrives even when the world feels unstable.

The Psychological Toll of Shutdowns

Shutdowns disrupt routines, and disrupted routines create instability in the mind. Common reactions include:

- **Anxiety:** Worrying constantly about money, food, housing, or safety.
- **Depression:** Feeling helpless, stuck, or paralyzed by circumstances beyond your control.
- **Family tension:** Stress can manifest as arguments, blame, or emotional withdrawal.
- **Isolation:** Fear and shame often cause people to pull away from their support systems.

Understanding these responses is the first step toward managing them. You are not "failing" if you feel anxious or down—you are experiencing a natural human reaction to instability. The goal is not to avoid these feelings but to channel them into constructive action.

Grounding Exercises: Reclaiming the Present

When the future feels uncertain, the present moment is your anchor. Grounding techniques calm the nervous system and keep the mind from spiraling.

1. The 5–4–3–2–1 Exercise

- Identify **5 things you can see**
- Identify **4 things you can touch**
- Identify **3 things you can hear**
- Identify **2 things you can smell**
- Identify **1 thing you can taste**

This simple practice interrupts racing thoughts and returns you to the here and now.

2. Breath Reset

- Inhale deeply for 4 counts.
- Hold for 4 counts.
- Exhale slowly for 6–8 counts.
- Repeat for at least 3–5 cycles.

Extending the exhale slows the heart rate and tells the body it is safe.

3. Body Scan

- Close your eyes and mentally "scan" your body from head to toe.
- Notice tension (tight shoulders, clenched jaw, restless legs).
- On each exhale, imagine releasing that tension into the ground.

Journaling Prompts: Writing Your Way Through Uncertainty

Journaling is a powerful psychological tool during shutdowns. It transforms overwhelming worries into structured reflections and actionable insights.

Prompts to Begin With:

1. *What is within my control right now?*
2. *What resources or strengths do I already have to draw on?*
3. *If I imagine my life six months from now, what do I want to remember about how I handled this?*
4. *Who in my community could I reach out to for support, and how might I support them in return?*
5. *What one small action can I take today to create stability?*

Even 5–10 minutes of writing daily can shift perspective from helplessness to empowerment.

Community Check-Ins: Breaking Isolation

Shutdown stress thrives in isolation. People often feel embarrassed to admit they're struggling, but silence magnifies the burden. Community check-ins—formal or informal—are essential.

1. Accountability Partners

Choose a friend or family member to check in with once a day or week. Share your challenges and your wins, no matter how small.

2. Support Circles

Neighborhood groups, faith communities, and online forums often host discussions or resource-sharing sessions during shutdowns. These provide not only practical help but emotional solidarity.

3. Mutual Aid Networks

Grassroots groups that share food, money, or services can double as emotional lifelines. Contributing—even in small ways—gives a sense of agency and belonging.

4. Family Routines

For parents, creating family rituals—shared meals, walks, or bedtime stories—anchors children emotionally and reduces their anxiety.

Reframing Shutdowns: From Crisis to Training Ground

Resilience is not about ignoring hardship but about transforming perspective. Shutdowns can be reframed as opportunities to:

- Practice patience and adaptability.
- Strengthen self-awareness and emotional regulation.
- Deepen bonds with family, friends, and neighbors.
- Discover hidden strengths you may not otherwise have tapped.

Every shutdown becomes a test run for resilience—an exercise in emotional fitness that builds confidence for future challenges.

Practical Mental Health Resources

- **Free hotlines:** National Suicide Prevention Lifeline (988), Veterans Crisis Line, and local hotlines remain active even during shutdowns.
- **Community health centers:** Many clinics offer free or low-cost counseling.
- **Telehealth apps:** Even if insurance is disrupted, affordable options exist for virtual therapy.
- **Peer support groups:** Online forums and local community meetings provide shared space for venting and advice.

Looking Ahead

Shutdowns may disrupt paychecks, benefits, and services, but they do not have to break your spirit. By practicing grounding, journaling, and community check-ins, you can stay emotionally centered and mentally strong. Resilience is a skill set—one that grows each time you face uncertainty with intention and courage.

Key Takeaways from Chapter 8

- Shutdowns trigger anxiety, depression, family tension, and isolation.
- Grounding exercises (5–4–3–2–1, breath reset, body scan) restore calm in the moment.
- Journaling helps process emotions and identify actionable steps.
- Community check-ins reduce isolation and strengthen resilience networks.
- Reframing shutdowns as training grounds for resilience builds long-term psychological strength.
- Free hotlines, clinics, and peer groups provide crucial mental health support.

Chapter 9: Building Mutual Aid Networks

When official systems stall, the most reliable support often comes not from agencies or programs, but from the people right next door. Shutdowns reveal a basic truth: our greatest source of resilience lies in community. **Mutual aid networks**—grassroots groups where neighbors pool resources and share skills—become lifelines when federal and state safety nets weaken.

This chapter explores how to build and sustain hyperlocal safety nets for food, childcare, and healthcare. By forming intentional, cooperative support systems, individuals can transform isolation into collective strength.

What is Mutual Aid?

Mutual aid is not charity. It is not about one group "helping" another from above—it is about reciprocity. In a mutual aid network:

- Everyone has something to give, whether food, skills, time, or emotional support.
- Everyone has the right to receive when in need.
- Relationships are built on trust, dignity, and cooperation rather than hierarchy.

Historically, mutual aid has appeared during wars, economic crises, pandemics, and natural disasters. Shutdowns are another kind of disruption, and the same principle applies: when institutions pause, communities step forward.

Why Mutual Aid During Shutdowns?

Shutdowns don't just halt government paychecks; they ripple into food stamps, housing vouchers, school meals, and healthcare approvals. Mutual aid counters those ripple effects by:

- **Filling gaps** when programs like SNAP, WIC, or Section 8 pause.
- **Reducing isolation** by bringing neighbors together.
- **Pooling resources** so that one household's surplus offsets another's shortage.
- **Building resilience** that lasts beyond the shutdown, creating networks for everyday life.

Step One: Mapping Your Community

The first step in building a mutual aid network is understanding who is around you and what they can contribute.

1. Identify Participants

- Start with family, friends, neighbors, or coworkers.
- Use local spaces (libraries, community centers, places of worship, neighborhood associations) to find interested people.

2. Map Needs and Skills

Create a simple chart:

- Needs: childcare, groceries, medicine pickups, transportation, housing support.
- Skills: cooking, repairs, teaching, medical knowledge, access to vehicles.

3. Establish Contact Points

Set up a shared communication system: a group text thread, a WhatsApp group, a Facebook group, or a neighborhood bulletin board. Accessibility is key—choose what works for your community.

Step Two: Organizing Food Support

Food insecurity is one of the most pressing challenges during a shutdown. Mutual aid food systems can be simple yet powerful.

1. Meal Rotations

- Families take turns preparing large meals to share among households.
- Rotations reduce costs and spread effort across the group.

2. Community Pantries

- Establish a "take what you need, give what you can" pantry in a central location (porch, garage, community center).
- Stock with shelf-stable goods like rice, beans, pasta, and canned vegetables.

3. Garden Networks

- Share backyard harvests or start community gardens.
- Even small container gardens can contribute herbs, greens, and vegetables.

Step Three: Childcare Solutions

When Head Start programs or school systems cut hours due to funding, parents scramble for childcare. Mutual aid circles provide flexible, affordable solutions.

1. Parent Rotations

- Parents alternate supervising small groups of children, creating a co-op model.
- This allows parents to work, job-hunt, or rest while ensuring safe childcare.

2. Skill-Sharing Childcare

- Parents or neighbors with teaching or creative skills can host learning/play sessions.
- Kids benefit from structured activities while parents get relief.

3. Emergency Childcare Lists

- Create a roster of trusted adults available on short notice.
- This prevents parents from being forced into unsafe or expensive last-minute options.

Step Four: Healthcare Support

Shutdowns disrupt paperwork, approvals, and prescription systems. Mutual aid fills gaps with community-based care.

1. Medicine Pickup Networks

- Volunteers with reliable transportation pick up prescriptions for elderly or mobility-limited neighbors.

2. First Aid & Basic Care

- Identify individuals with healthcare training (nurses, EMTs, caregivers).
- Provide workshops on basic first aid, wound care, and chronic condition management.

3. Telehealth Knowledge Sharing

- Share lists of free or low-cost telehealth platforms.
- Pool funds to cover urgent virtual consultations when needed.

Step Five: Sustaining the Network

Mutual aid works best when built to last.

- **Regular Check-Ins:** Hold weekly or biweekly calls, meetups, or digital updates to assess needs and share wins.
- **Shared Leadership:** Avoid putting the burden on one organizer; rotate leadership and responsibilities.
- **Transparency:** Be clear about contributions and distributions—trust grows when everyone knows how resources are shared.
- **Celebrate Wins:** Acknowledge moments when the network helped someone—stories build morale and commitment.

Psychological Benefits of Mutual Aid

Mutual aid doesn't just meet physical needs—it heals emotional ones.

- **Reduces isolation:** Knowing someone cares creates emotional safety.
- **Restores dignity:** Families give as well as receive, avoiding the stigma of charity.
- **Builds empowerment:** Instead of waiting for stalled systems, communities take control of their own survival.

Shutdowns may create fear, but mutual aid builds solidarity—a reminder that no one is alone in crisis.

Looking Ahead

Mutual aid networks are one of the most powerful tools for surviving a shutdown. They transform disconnected households into resilient communities that can share food, childcare, and healthcare. While official systems may falter, grassroots cooperation keeps life moving.

Key Takeaways from Chapter 9

- Mutual aid is reciprocal, not hierarchical—everyone gives and receives.
- Mapping community needs and skills creates the foundation of a network.
- Food support (rotations, pantries, gardens) stabilizes households during SNAP/WIC delays.
- Childcare co-ops and emergency rosters prevent parental burnout.
- Healthcare support through pickups, first aid, and telehealth fills gaps when approvals stall.
- Sustaining mutual aid requires shared leadership, transparency, and storytelling.
- Beyond logistics, mutual aid provides dignity, solidarity, and hope during shutdown uncertainty.

Chapter 10: From Surviving to Thriving

By now, you've explored the anatomy of a shutdown, learned to stabilize your finances and food supply, protected your healthcare, cared for your family, and built support networks that extend beyond federal programs. But the ultimate goal of this book is not just to get you through the next shutdown. It is to reframe these disruptions as opportunities for transformation.

Shutdowns strip away the illusion of permanence in systems we take for granted. They reveal how fragile centralized structures can be—and how powerful individuals and communities become when they reclaim responsibility for their stability. This final chapter moves beyond survival tactics. It offers a framework for thriving: reducing dependency, strengthening resilience, and building personal sovereignty.

From Dependency to Independence

Many households operate under the assumption that government services will always function: benefits will load, checks will arrive, offices will process paperwork on schedule. Shutdowns expose the vulnerability of this assumption. True resilience requires shifting from dependency to independence wherever possible.

Practical Independence Steps:

- **Financial:** Diversify income streams, even if small, to reduce reliance on one paycheck or benefit program.
- **Food:** Build pantries, gardens, and food-sharing networks to keep nourishment in community hands.
- **Healthcare:** Keep a personal medical record, know your alternatives, and cultivate local networks of care.
- **Housing:** Strengthen communication with landlords, develop fallback plans, and explore co-housing or cooperative arrangements.

Each step toward independence creates a layer of security no shutdown can fully erase.

Building Resilience as a Skill

Resilience is not a personality trait—it is a practiced discipline. Just as muscles grow with training, resilience grows when you repeatedly adapt, recover, and innovate under pressure.

Resilience Practices:

1. **Scenario Planning:** Ask, *What if this service disappeared for three months? What would I do?*
2. **Micro-Reserves:** Keep small cushions in every category—food, cash, medicine, energy.
3. **Routine Stress Drills:** Occasionally "practice" life without a resource (cook only with pantry staples for a week, use cash instead of cards) to strengthen adaptability.
4. **Debriefing After Crises:** Reflect after each disruption—what worked, what failed, what can be improved.

Resilience is not about never feeling stress; it's about knowing you can bend without breaking.

Sovereignty: Reclaiming Authority Over Your Life

Sovereignty means having the ability to govern your own stability, rather than relying entirely on external systems. While no one can control every circumstance, you can reclaim authority in areas that matter most.

Sovereignty Frameworks:

- **Personal Sovereignty:** Taking ownership of your time, choices, and mindset.
- **Financial Sovereignty:** Creating streams of income not dictated solely by government or employer.
- **Community Sovereignty:** Building mutual aid circles where power and resources circulate locally.
- **Psychological Sovereignty:** Practicing grounding, reframing, and resilience tools to ensure your mind remains your own during crisis.

Sovereignty doesn't mean isolation. It means building strength within so that you can engage with systems on your terms, not as a powerless recipient.

Mindset Tools for Thriving

Shifting from survival mode to thriving requires a different lens. Instead of asking, *"How do I get through this?"* ask, *"What do I want to build from this?"*

Mindset Shifts:

- **Scarcity → Resourcefulness:** Focus on what you can do with what you already have.
- **Fear → Opportunity:** Each disruption exposes weak points you can now strengthen.
- **Isolation → Community:** The more you connect, the stronger everyone becomes.
- **Waiting → Acting:** Instead of waiting for systems to restart, take initiative in creating stability now.

Empowerment Frameworks

To integrate all the lessons from this book, here are three empowerment frameworks:

1. The Circle of Control

- *What I Control:* My spending, my preparedness, my outreach to community.
- *What I Influence:* My landlord negotiations, group networks, family resilience.
- *What I Cannot Control:* Congressional debates, federal office closures.

  Focus energy only on the first two rings. Release the third.

2. The Three Pillars of Resilience

1. **Preparedness** (resources and planning)
2. **Flexibility** (ability to pivot when systems stall)
3. **Connection** (community networks of support)

Thriving requires balancing all three—not just storing supplies but also cultivating adaptability and relationships.

3. The Resilience Ladder

Visualize your growth as climbing steps:

- Step 1: Stabilize essentials (food, housing, medicine).
- Step 2: Build buffers (small reserves, side income, fallback plans).
- Step 3: Create networks (mutual aid, community ties).
- Step 4: Practice sovereignty (independence in thought, action, and planning).
- Step 5: Thrive (using disruption as a launchpad for stronger, freer living).

Turning Crisis Into Catalyst

Shutdowns are political deadlocks, but for citizens they can be catalysts for evolution. Each disruption offers a chance to strengthen systems at home and in community, test personal resilience, and develop sovereignty that endures beyond politics.

The question is no longer, *"What if the government shuts down?"* but *"How strong will I be when it does?"*

Key Takeaways from Chapter 10

- Shutdowns expose dependency but also provide opportunities to build independence.
- Resilience is a skill set: scenario planning, micro-reserves, and stress drills sharpen adaptability.
- Sovereignty means reclaiming authority over your financial, personal, and community stability.
- Mindset tools transform fear into action, scarcity into resourcefulness, and isolation into connection.
- Empowerment frameworks (Circle of Control, Three Pillars, Resilience Ladder) provide practical ways to thrive.
- Every shutdown can serve as a training ground for becoming stronger, freer, and more resilient than before.

Appendix A: Essential Shutdown Survival Checklists

Preparedness is easiest to practice when it is practical. To help you immediately apply the lessons of this book, the following checklists provide step-by-step tools for food, water, paperwork, benefits, and budgeting. Print or copy these pages, keep them in a binder or folder, and update them regularly. During a shutdown, they become your quick-reference survival kit.

1. Food & Water Stockpile List

A shutdown may not close grocery stores, but benefit delays or lost income can limit your access to them. Maintaining a modest, rotating stockpile ensures you never face an empty pantry.

Pantry Staples (2–4 weeks minimum):

- Grains: rice (white or brown), oats, pasta, quinoa, flour, tortillas
- Legumes: lentils, black beans, chickpeas, split peas, canned beans
- Proteins: canned tuna/chicken/salmon, peanut butter, powdered milk, shelf-stable tofu
- Vegetables: canned tomatoes, corn, peas, carrots, green beans, mixed veg
- Fruits: dried fruit (raisins, apricots, cranberries), canned fruit, applesauce cups
- Fats & oils: olive oil, vegetable oil, coconut oil, shelf-stable butter/ghee
- Flavor: salt, sugar, bouillon cubes, spices, vinegar, soy sauce
- Miscellaneous: crackers, instant soups, granola bars, shelf-stable meal packs

Frozen Goods (if space available):

- Bread, tortillas, bagels
- Pre-cooked proteins (chicken, beef, beans)
- Vegetables (broccoli, spinach, peas, peppers)
- Batch-cooked meals (soups, casseroles, stews)

Water Supply:

- Store at least **1 gallon of water per person, per day** (minimum 7 days if possible).
- Consider extra water for pets, cooking, and hygiene.
- Keep a water filter (portable or pitcher-based) for emergencies.

Child & Infant Needs:

- Formula, baby food pouches, powdered milk
- Extra diapers, wipes, and rash cream

2. Critical Document Tracker

During shutdowns, processing delays can create backlogs. Having your documents organized ensures you can provide proof of eligibility, identity, or financial need at a moment's notice.

Create a folder (physical and digital) with copies of:

- Government ID: driver's license, passport, state ID
- Social Security card
- Birth certificates (for all household members)
- Medical insurance cards, Medicare/Medicaid documents
- Veterans benefits ID and service records
- Housing lease or mortgage agreement
- Recent utility bills (proof of address)
- Tax returns (last 2 years)
- SNAP/WIC eligibility letters
- SSI/SSDI approval letters
- HUD/Section 8 paperwork
- Employment verification/pay stubs (if applicable)

Tips:

- Keep one hard copy in a fireproof folder.
- Scan and store encrypted digital versions (on a secure cloud or flash drive).
- Update annually or after major life changes.

3. Benefits Contact Sheet

When benefits stall, knowing exactly who to call (and having all reference numbers handy) can save hours of frustration. Fill out this contact sheet and keep it updated.

Program	Contact Info	Case/Account Number	Notes
SSI / SSDI	Social Security Administration: 1-800-772-1213	____________ ____________	Local office: ________________ ________
SNAP	State SNAP hotline: ________________ ________	____________ ____________	Caseworker name: ________________ ________
WIC	Local WIC office phone: ________________ ________	____________ ____________	Clinic location: ________________ ________
Medicare	Medicare: 1-800-633-4227	____________ ____________	Part A / B / D info: ________________ ________
Medicaid	State Medicaid office: ________________ ________	____________ ____________	Caseworker name: ________________ ________

Program	Contact Info	Case/Account Number	Notes
VA Benefits	VA hotline: 1-800-827-1000	____________ ____________	Local VA office: ________________ ________
HUD / Section 8	Local housing authority: ________________ ________	____________ ____________	Caseworker name: ________________ ________
Unemployment	State unemployment office: ________________ ________	____________ ____________	Filing website: ________________ ________
Local Aid	Food bank: ________________ ________	____________ ____________	Community aid group: ________________ ________

Tip: Post a copy of this sheet near your phone or in your survival binder.

4. Emergency Budget Template

When shutdowns disrupt income or benefits, you may need to operate on a lean emergency budget. Use this template to track essentials and cut non-essentials.

Step 1: Income During Shutdown

- Savings available: $____________
- Side hustle/gig income: $____________
- Benefits (if still arriving): $____________
- Family/friend support: $____________
  Total: $____________

Step 2: Priority Expenses (List Minimums)

- Rent/Mortgage: $____________
- Utilities (water, electricity, gas, phone): $____________
- Food/Groceries: $____________
- Transportation (gas, bus, car payment, insurance): $____________
- Medical (prescriptions, copays): $____________
- Childcare/Education: $____________
  Total Essentials: $____________

Step 3: Secondary Expenses (Reduce/Defer if Needed)

- Internet / Streaming / Subscriptions: $____________
- Clothing / Household goods: $____________
- Entertainment: $____________
- Debt repayment (contact lenders for deferment if needed): $____________

Step 4: Adjustments & Notes

- Areas I can reduce: ______________________________
- Areas I must protect: ______________________________
- Emergency cutoff point (the minimum I need per month): $____________

Closing Note

Checklists don't remove the challenges of a shutdown, but they reduce the chaos. By knowing what food you have, where your documents are, who to contact, and how to adjust your budget, you transform shutdown stress into organized action. Keep these tools visible and updated—they are your first line of defense when official systems slow down.

Appendix B: Resource & Rights Directory

When shutdowns drag on, the most stressful part is often not knowing where to turn. Delays in benefits, closed offices, and confusing messages from agencies can leave families in limbo. This appendix provides a practical directory of resources and rights so that you can move from uncertainty to action.

Keep this section printed, bookmarked, or saved offline. It gives you access points to federal contingency plans, nonprofit lifelines, online tools, and the basic rights you hold as a citizen when programs stall.

1. Federal Agency Shutdown Contingency Links

Every major federal agency publishes a "shutdown contingency plan" outlining what will continue and what will pause. These resources may shift depending on the year, but the following starting points remain consistent:

- **Office of Management and Budget (OMB)**: https://www.whitehouse.gov/omb/ (Houses all official agency shutdown contingency plans in one place.)
- **Social Security Administration (SSA):** https://www.ssa.gov/news/ (Updates on SSI, SSDI, and Social Security operations during funding gaps.)
- **U.S. Department of Agriculture (USDA – SNAP, WIC):** https://www.fns.usda.gov/ (Guidance on food programs, including contingency funds for SNAP and WIC.)
- **Department of Veterans Affairs (VA):** https://www.va.gov/opa/ (Explains which services remain active at VA hospitals and which benefits may slow.)
- **Department of Housing and Urban Development (HUD):** https://www.hud.gov/ (Information on Section 8, housing assistance payments, and HUD-funded programs.)
- **Centers for Medicare & Medicaid Services (CMS):** https://www.cms.gov/ (Details on Medicare/Medicaid coverage, claims processing, and delays.)

- **Internal Revenue Service (IRS):**
  https://www.irs.gov/
  (Announcements on tax refund processing and agency closures.)

2. Nonprofit and Community Aid Organizations

When official systems pause, nonprofits and charities step in to fill the gaps. These organizations operate nationally and locally:

Food Assistance

- **Feeding America:** https://www.feedingamerica.org/
  (National food bank locator for immediate meal support.)
- **Meals on Wheels:** https://www.mealsonwheelsamerica.org/
  (Meal delivery for seniors and vulnerable adults.)

Housing & Utility Assistance

- **National Low Income Housing Coalition (NLIHC):** https://nlihc.org/
  (Tracks housing rights, emergency rental assistance, and eviction defense resources.)
- **United Way 211:** Dial **2-1-1** or visit https://www.211.org/
  (A national hotline connecting you to local rental, utility, and emergency aid.)

Healthcare & Medicine

- **National Association of Free & Charitable Clinics:** https://nafcclinics.org/
  (Directory of free and low-cost community health clinics.)
- **NeedyMeds:** https://www.needymeds.org/
  (Prescription assistance programs and drug discount resources.)

Financial & General Assistance

- **The Salvation Army:** https://www.salvationarmyusa.org/
  (Emergency shelter, meals, and financial relief programs.)
- **Catholic Charities USA:** https://www.catholiccharitiesusa.org/
  (Non-denominational community aid, including food, housing, and childcare.)

3. Online Tools for Legal Aid, Housing, and Benefits Tracking

Technology can simplify the chaos of shutdowns by helping you track applications, access free legal advice, and monitor housing or benefits status.

Legal Aid

- **Legal Services Corporation (LSC):** https://www.lsc.gov/find-legal-aid
  (Free or low-cost legal help for tenants, benefits disputes, and consumer issues.)
- **LawHelp.org:** https://www.lawhelp.org/
  (State-specific legal aid resources searchable by topic.)

Housing & Benefits Tracking

- **Benefits.gov:** https://www.benefits.gov/
  (Central portal for federal benefits and eligibility updates.)
- **HUD Resource Locator:** https://resources.hud.gov/
  (Search for local HUD offices and housing authorities.)

Healthcare

- **Healthcare.gov:** https://www.healthcare.gov/
  (Updates on federal health insurance marketplace operations.)
- **GoodRx:** https://www.goodrx.com/
  (Compare prescription prices and find discounts.)

4. Citizen's Rights When Benefits Are Delayed

Even during shutdowns, you retain important legal rights. Understanding them ensures you can advocate for yourself and your family.

1. Right to Appeal

If your SNAP, SSI, or other benefits are denied or delayed, you still have the right to file an appeal—even if processing is delayed. File early to secure your place in the queue.

2. Right to Documentation

You can request written explanations from agencies about why benefits are paused or denied. These letters are crucial when negotiating with landlords, utility companies, or creditors.

3. Tenant Rights

- Landlords cannot legally evict you overnight without due process.
- Many states require **written notice periods** and formal court proceedings.
- If your rent is delayed due to Section 8 or HUD subsidy pauses, you may be entitled to legal protections depending on state law.

4. Utility Protections

In some states, utilities cannot be shut off during periods of declared hardship. Call your utility company and request a **hardship protection plan.**

5. Credit & Debt Protections

- Contact creditors early: many offer temporary deferments during shutdowns.
- You have the right to request that late payments be marked as hardship-related, not as defaults, if they are linked to benefit delays.

6. Workplace Rights for Federal Employees

- Furloughed workers cannot be forced to work without pay unless designated "essential."
- Federal employees are entitled to back pay once the shutdown ends. Contractors, however, may not be guaranteed back pay.

Final Note

This directory is not exhaustive, but it provides a strong foundation. Federal contingency links tell you what's officially paused. Nonprofits and online tools fill in the gaps. And knowing your rights ensures that when benefits are delayed, you remain empowered to defend your stability.

Shutdowns may interrupt systems—but they do not erase your rights, nor your access to community-driven solutions. Keep this appendix close. It is your map when official roads close.

Appendix C: 30-Day Shutdown Action Plan

Surviving a government shutdown is about more than reacting to each day's headlines. The most effective approach is structured action: breaking down the uncertainty into daily steps that build security, reduce stress, and protect your family. This 30-day plan provides a framework for the first month of a shutdown, turning chaos into order.

Use this appendix as a **roadmap**—adapt as needed based on your household size, benefits, and community resources.

Week 1: Stabilize the Foundations (Days 1–7)

Day 1 – Take Inventory

- Review pantry, freezer, and water supplies.
- Check prescription counts and refill if eligible.
- List upcoming bills and due dates.
- Gather all critical documents into one folder (see Appendix A).

Day 2 – Secure Cash Flow

- Withdraw a small amount of cash for essentials (ATMs may become harder to access if networks strain).
- Adjust household budget using the Emergency Budget Template.
- Identify one or two potential side-income or barter opportunities.

Day 3 – Contact Benefits Agencies

- Call SSA, SNAP office, Medicaid, or HUD to ask about your case status.
- Document any delays in writing.
- Update your Benefits Contact Sheet (Appendix A).

Day 4 – Set Up Food Resilience

- Organize pantry by categories: proteins, grains, vegetables, snacks.
- Begin a rotation plan (oldest items eaten first).
- Identify a local food pantry or Feeding America partner.

Day 5 – Build Communication Networks

- Start or join a neighborhood group chat (WhatsApp, text chain, Facebook group).
- Share contact info with at least 2 trusted neighbors for mutual aid.

Day 6 – Healthcare Check-In

- Schedule pending medical appointments before backlogs worsen.
- Ask your provider about a 90-day prescription supply.
- Identify nearest urgent care or low-cost clinic.

Day 7 – Family Stability Day

- Create a family meeting: explain shutdown in simple, calm terms.
- Establish routines for meals, schoolwork, and relaxation.
- Write down childcare backup options.

Week 2: Build Buffers (Days 8–14)

Day 8 – Food Stock-Up

- Use available benefits or cash to purchase low-cost bulk staples (beans, rice, oats, flour).
- Freeze bread and proteins for later weeks.

Day 9 – Utilities & Rent/Housing

- Call landlord, mortgage lender, or utility companies.
- Ask about hardship options, extensions, or deferrals.
- Document all agreements in writing.

Day 10 – Expand Support Network

- Identify at least one local nonprofit for food or rental assistance.
- Share resource info with neighbors or friends.

Day 11 – Start Side Hustle or Barter Plan

- Sign up for at least one gig app, or propose a barter exchange (childcare for groceries, repairs for meals).
- Set a realistic weekly income/barter goal.

Day 12 – Emotional Resilience Practice

- Try a new grounding technique (breathing, body scan, 5–4–3–2–1).
- Begin journaling 5 minutes a day with prompts from Chapter 8.

Day 13 – Check Transportation Resilience

- Fill up gas tank or charge transit card.
- Plan backup routes if services reduce.
- Carpool with neighbors if needed.

Day 14 – Community Meal

- Organize a shared meal with friends, neighbors, or family.
- Reinforce bonds and reduce isolation.

Week 3: Strengthen Systems (Days 15–21)
Day 15 – Review Progress

- Revisit budget. Adjust based on actual spending.
- Take inventory of food and supplies again.

Day 16 – Strengthen Food Plan

- Batch cook meals to stretch ingredients.
- Freeze leftovers for later weeks.

Day 17 – Mutual Aid Expansion

- Host a mini check-in with your local network.
- Share skills (teaching, repairs, cooking).
- Set up a rotating childcare or meal plan if not already done.

Day 18 – Healthcare Resilience II

- Confirm medication refills are on track.
- Ask providers about generic or over-the-counter substitutes.
- Share clinic/telehealth info with network.

Day 19 – Household Maintenance

- Fix small repairs now to avoid bigger costs later.
- Swap tools or supplies with neighbors to save money.

Day 20 – Rights & Legal Readiness

- Review your tenant or worker rights (see Appendix B).
- Contact local legal aid or tenant groups if eviction threats arise.

Day 21 – Mental Health Recharge

- Plan a low-cost "family fun day" (picnic, board games, storytelling).
- Balance survival tasks with joy-building moments.

Week 4: Adapt & Empower (Days 22–30)

Day 22 – Evaluate Income Options

- Assess gig/barter income.
- Identify ways to expand (e.g., tutoring, local babysitting, online sales).

Day 23 – Long-Term Food Strategy

- Begin small gardening project (herbs, greens in containers).
- Swap recipes and food prep strategies in your network.

Day 24 – Utility Backup

- Purchase candles, rechargeable lights, or solar chargers.
- Stock extra batteries.

Day 25 – Community Aid Outreach

- Volunteer or contribute to a food pantry or aid group (even small contributions matter).
- Build reciprocal goodwill for when you may need help later.

Day 26 – Resilience Reflection

- Journal: *What did I learn this month about my strengths?*
- Identify weak points that need strengthening.

Day 27 – Emergency Simulation

- Try a 24-hour "shutdown drill" at home (use only pantry food, no internet/TV).
- Debrief with your family afterward: what worked, what needs fixing.

Day 28 – Legal/Financial Check-In

- Call creditors again if needed; request extensions.
- Reassess emergency cash or savings status.

Day 29 – Share Knowledge

- Teach at least one neighbor, friend, or relative something you've learned (budgeting, food prep, healthcare backup).
- Resilience grows when knowledge is shared.

Day 30 – Celebrate Survival & Plan for Thriving

- Host a reflection meeting with family or network.
- Write down the systems you've built and commit to maintaining them beyond the shutdown.
- Reframe the past 30 days as a training ground—not just survival, but sovereignty.

Closing Note

The 30-day shutdown action plan is not just about getting through the month—it's about building long-term stability. Each daily step is a brick in a larger foundation: one where you rely less on fragile systems and more on your resourcefulness, community, and resilience. By following this roadmap, you move from reactive survival to proactive empowerment.

Message from the Author:

I hope you enjoyed this book, I love astrology and knew there was not a book such as this out on the shelf. I love metaphysical items as well. Please check out my other books:

-Life of Government Benefits

-My life of Hell

-My life with Hydrocephalus

-Red Sky

-World Domination:Woman's rule

-World Domination:Woman's Rule 2: The War

-Life and Banishment of Apophis: book 1

-The Kidney Friendly Diet

-The Ultimate Hemp Cookbook

-Creating a Dispensary(legally)

-Cleanliness throughout life: the importance of showering from childhood to adulthood.

-Strong Roots: The Risks of Overcoddling children

-Hemp Horoscopes: Cosmic Insights and Earthly Healing

- Celestial Hemp Navigating the Zodiac: Through the Green Cosmos

-Astrological Hemp: Aligning The Stars with Earth's Ancient Herb

-The Astrological Guide to Hemp: Stars, Signs, and Sacred Leaves

-Green Growth: Innovative Marketing Strategies for your Hemp Products and Dispensary

-Cosmic Cannabis

-Astrological Munchies

-Henry The Hemp

-Zodiacal Roots: The Astrological Soul Of Hemp

- **Green Constellations: Intersection of Hemp and Zodiac**

-Hemp in The Houses: An astrological Adventure Through The Cannabis Galaxy

-Galactic Ganja Guide
Heavenly Hemp
Zodiac Leaves
Doctor Who Astrology
Cannastrology
Stellar Satvias and Cosmic Indicas
Celestial Cannabis: A Zodiac Journey
AstroHerbology: The Sky and The Soil: Volume 1
AstroHerbology:Celestial Cannabis:Volume 2
Cosmic Cannabis Cultivation
The Starry Guide to Herbal Harmony: Volume 1
The Starry Guide to Herbal Harmony: Cannabis Universe: Volume 2
Yugioh Astrology: Astrological Guide to Deck, Duels and more
Nightmare Mansion: Echoes of The Abyss
Nightmare Mansion 2: Legacy of Shadows
Nightmare Mansion 3: Shadows of the Forgotten
Nightmare Mansion 4: Echoes of the Damned
The Life and Banishment of Apophis: Book 2
Nightmare Mansion: Halls of Despair
Healing with Herb: Cannabis and Hydrocephalus
Planetary Pot: Aligning with Astrological Herbs: Volume 1
Fast Track to Freedom: 30 Days to Financial Independence Using AI, Assets, and Agile Hustles
Cosmic Hemp Pathways
How to Become Financially Free in 30 Days: 10,000 Paths to Prosperity
Zodiacal Herbage: Astrological Insights: Volume 1
Nightmare Mansion: Whispers in the Walls
The Daleks Invade Atlantis
Henry the hemp and Hydrocephalus

10X The Kidney Friendly Diet

Cannabis Universe: Adult coloring book

Hemp Astrology: The Healing Power of the Stars

Zodiacal Herbage: Astrological Insights: Cannabis Universe: Volume 2

Planetary Pot: Aligning with Astrological Herbs: Cannabis Universes: Volume 2

Doctor Who: Convergence Protocol – The Replicator War

Nightmare Mansion: Curse of the Blood Moon

The Celestial Stoner: A Guide to the Zodiac

Cosmic Pleasures: Sex Toy Astrology for Every Sign

Hydrocephalus Astrology: Navigating the Stars and Healing Waters

Lapis and the Mischievous Chocolate Bar

Celestial Positions: Sexual Astrology for Every Sign

Apophis's Shadow Work Journal: **:** A Journey of Self-Discovery and Healing

Kinky Cosmos: Sexual Kink Astrology for Every Sign

Digital Cosmos: The Astrological Digimon Compendium

Stellar Seeds: The Cosmic Guide to Growing with Astrology

Apophis's Daily Gratitude Journal

Cat Astrology: Feline Mysteries of the Cosmos

The Cosmic Kama Sutra: An Astrological Guide to Sexual Positions

Unleash Your Potential: A Guided Journal Powered by AI Insights

Whispers of the Enchanted Grove

Cosmic Pleasures: An Astrological Guide to Sexual Kinks

369, 12 Manifestation Journal

Whisper of the nocturne journal(blank journal for writing or drawing)

The Boogey Book

Locked In Reflection: A Chastity Journey Through Locktober

Generating Wealth Quickly:How to Generate $100,000 in 24 Hours

Star Magic: Harness the Power of the Universe

The Flatulence Chronicles: A Fart Journal for Self-Discovery

The Doctor and The Death Moth

Seize the Day: A Personal Seizure Tracking Journal

The Ultimate Boogeyman Safari: A Journey into the Boogie World and Beyond

Whispers of Samhain: 1,000 Spells of Love, Luck, and Lunar Magic: Samhain Spell Book

Apophis's guides:Witch's Spellbook Crafting Guide for Halloween

Frost & Flame: The Enchanted Yule Grimoire of 1000 Winter Spells

The Ultimate Boogey Goo Guide & Spooky Activities for Halloween Fun

Harmony of the Scales: A Libra's Spellcraft for Balance and Beauty

The Enchanted Advent: 36 Days of Christmas Wonders

Nightmare Mansion: The Labyrinth of Screams

Harvest of Enchantment: 1,000 Spells of Gratitude, Love, and Fortune for Thanksgiving

The Boogey Chronicles: A Journal of Nightly Encounters and Shadowy Secrets

The 12 Days of Financial Freedom: A Step-by-Step Christmas Countdown to Transform Your Finances

Sigil of the Eternal Spiral Blank Journal

A Christmas Feast: Timeless Recipes for Every Meal

Holiday Stress-Free Solutions: A Survival Guide to Thriving During the Festive Season

Yu-Gi-Oh! Holiday Gifting Mastery: The Ultimate Guide for Fans and Newcomers Alike

Holiday Harmony: A Hydrocephalus Survival Guide for the Festive Season

Celestial Craft: The Witch's Almanac for 2025 – A Cosmic Guide to Manifestations, Moons, and Mystical Events

Doctor Who: The Toymaker's Winter Wonderland

Tulsa King Unveiled: A Thrilling Guide to Stallone's Mafia Masterpiece

Pendulum Craft: A Complete Guide to Crafting and Using Personalized Divination Tools

Nightmare Mansion: Santa's Eternal Eve

Starlight Noel: A Cosmic Journey through Christmas Mysteries

The Dark Architect: Unlocking the Blueprint of Existence

Surviving the Embrace: The Ultimate Guide to Encounters with The Hugging Molly

The Enchanted Codex: Secrets of the Craft for Witches, Wiccans, and Pagans

Harvest of Gratitude: A Complete Thanksgiving Guide

Yuletide Essentials: A Complete Guide to an Authentic and Magical Christmas

Celestial Smokes: A Cosmic Guide to Cigars and Astrology

Living in Balance: A Comprehensive Survival Guide to Thriving with Diabetes Insipidus

Cosmic Symbiosis: The Venom Zodiac Chronicles

The Cursed Paw of Ambition

Cosmic Symbiosis: The Astrological Venom Journal

Celestial Wonders Unfold: A Stargazer's Guide to the Cosmos (2024-2029)

The Ultimate Black Friday Prepper's Guide: Mastering Shopping Strategies and Savings

Cosmic Sales: The Astrological Guide to Black Friday Shopping

Legends of the Corn Mother and Other Harvest Myths

Whispers of the Harvest: The Corn Mother's Journal

The Evergreen Spellbook

The Doctor Meets the Boogeyman

The White Witch of Rose Hall's SpellBook

The Gingerbread Golem's Shadow: A Study in Sweet Darkness

The Gingerbread Golem Codex: An Academic Exploration of Sweet Myths

The Gingerbread Golem Grimoire: Sweet Magicks and Spells for the Festive Witch

The Curse of the Gingerbread Golem

10-minute Christmas Crafts for kids

Christmas Crisis Solutions: The Ultimate Last-Minute Survival Guide

Gingerbread Golem Recipes: Holiday Treats with a Magical Twist

The Infinite Key: Unlocking Mystical Secrets of the Ages

Enchanted Yule: A Wiccan and Pagan Guide to a Magical and Memorable Season

Dinosaurs of Power: Unlocking Ancient Magick

Astro-Dinos: The Cosmic Guide to Prehistoric Wisdom

Gallifrey's Yule Logs: A Festive Doctor Who Cookbook

The Dino Grimoire: Secrets of Prehistoric Magick

The Gift They Never Knew They Needed

The Gingerbread Golem's Culinary Alchemy: Enchanting Recipes for a Sweetly Dark Feast

A Time Lord Christmas: Holiday Adventures with the Doctor

Krampusproofing Your Home: Defensive Strategies for Yule

Silent Frights: A Collection of Christmas Creepypastas to Chill Your Bones

Santa Raptor's Jolly Carnage: A Dino-Claus Christmas Tale

Prehistoric Palettes: A Dino Wicca Coloring Journey

The Christmas Wishkeeper Chronicles

The Starlight Sleigh: A Holiday Journey

Elf Secrets: The True Magic of the North Pole

Candy Cane Conjurations

Cooking with Kids: Recipes Under 20 Minutes

Doctor Who: The TARDIS Confiscation

The Anxiety First Aid Kit: Quick Tools to Calm Your Mind

Frosty Whispers: A Winter's Tale

The Infinite Key: Unlocking the Secrets to Prosperity, Resilience, and Purpose

The Grasping Void: Why You'll Regret This Purchase

Astrology for Busy Bees: Star Signs Simplified

The Instant Focus Formula: Cut Through the Noise

The Secret Language of Colors: Unlocking the Emotional Codes

Sacred Fossil Chronicles: Blank Journal

The Christmas Cottage Miracle

Feeding Frenzy: Graboid-Inspired Recipes

Manifest in Minutes: The Quick Law of Attraction Guide

The Symbiote Chronicles: Doctor Who's Venomous Journey

Think Tiny, Grow Big: The Minimalist Mindset

The Energy Key: Unlocking Limitless Motivation

New Year, New Magic: Manifesting Your Best Year Yet

Unstoppable You: Mastering Confidence in Minutes

Infinite Energy: The Secret to Never Feeling Drained

Lightning Focus: Mastering the Art of Productivity in a Distracted World

Saturnalia Manifestation Magick: A Guide to Unlocking Abundance During the Solstice

Graboids and Garland: The Ultimate Tremors-Themed Christmas Guide

12 Nights of Holiday Magic

The Power of Pause: 60-Second Mindfulness Practices

The Quick Reset: How to Reclaim Your Life After Burnout

The Shadow Eater: A Tale of Despair and Survival

The Micro-Mastery Method: Transform Your Skills in Just Minutes a Day

Reclaiming Time: How to Live More by Doing Less
Chronovore: The Eternal Nexus
The Mind Reset: Unlocking Your Inner Peace in a Chaotic World
Confidence Code: Building Unshakable Self-Belief
Baby the Vampire Terrier
Baby the Vampire Terrier's Christmas Adventure
Celestial Streams: The Content Creator's Astrology Manual
The Wealth Whisperer: Unlocking Abundance with Everyday Actions
The Energy Equation: Maximize Your Output Without Burning Out
The Happiness Algorithm: Science-Backed Steps to Joyful Living
Stress-Free Success: Achieving Goals Without Anxiety
Mindful Wealth: The New Blueprint for Financial Freedom
The Festive Flavors of New Year: A Culinary Celebration
The Master's Gambit: Keys of Eternal Power
Shadowed Secrets: Groundhog Day Mysteries
Beneath the Burrow: Lessons from the Groundhog
Spring's Whispers: The Groundhog's Prediction
The Limitless Mindset: Unlock Your Untapped Potential
The Focus Funnel: How to Cut Through Chaos and Get Results
Bold Moves: Building Courage to Live on Your Terms
The Daily Shift: Simple Practices for Lasting Transformation
The Quarter-Life Reset: Thriving in Your 20s and 30s
The Art of Shadowplay: Building Your Own Personal Myth
The Eternal Loop: Finding Purpose in Repetition
Burrowing Wisdom: Life Lessons from the Groundhog
Shadow Work: A Groundhog Day Perspective
Love in Bloom: 5-Minute Romantic Gestures
The Shadowspell Codex: Secrets of Forbidden Magick
The Burnout Cure: Finding Balance in a Busy World
The Groundhog Prophecy: Unlocking Seasonal Secrets
Nog Tales: The Spirited History of Eggnog

Six More Weeks: Embracing Seasonal Transitions
The Lumivian Chronicles: Fragments of the Fifth Dimension
Money on Your Mind: A Beginner's Guide to Wealth
The Focus Fix: Breaking Through Distraction
January's Spirit Keepers: Mystical Protectors of the Cold
Creativity Unchained: Unlocking Your Wildest Ideas in 2025
Manifestation Mastery: 365 Days to Rewrite Your Reality
The Groundhog's Mirror: Reflecting on Change
The Weeping Angels' Christmas Curse
Burrowed in Time: A Groundhog Day Journey
Heartbeats: Poems to Share with Your Valentine
Dino Wicca: The Sacred Grimoire of Prehistoric Magick
Courage of the Pride: Finding Your Inner Roar
The Lion's Leap: Bold Moves for Big Results
Healthy Hustle: Achieving Without Overworking
Practical Manifesting: Turning Dreams into Reality in 2025
Jurassic Pharaohs: Unlocking the Magick of Ancient Egypt and Dino Wicca
The Happiness Equation: Small Changes for Big Joy
The Confidence Compass: Finding Your Inner Strength
Whispers in the Hollow: Tales of the Forgotten Beasts
Echoes from the Hollow: The Return of Forgotten Beasts
The Hollow Ascendant: The Rise of the Forgotten Beasts
The Relationship Reset: Building Better Connections
Mastering the Morning: How to Win the Day Before 8 AM
The Shadow's Dance: Groundhog Day Symbolism
Cupid's Kitchen: Quick Valentine's Day Recipes
Valentine's Day on a Budget: Love Without Breaking the Bank
Astrocraft: Aligning the Stars in the World of Minecraft
Forecasting Life: Groundhog Day Reflections
Bleeding Hearts: Twisted Tales of Valentine's Terror
Herbal Smoke Revolution: The Ultimate Guide to Nature's Cigarette Alternative

Winter's Wrath: The Complete Survival Blueprint for Extreme Freezes.

The Groundhog's Shadow: A Tale of Seasons

Burrowed Insights: Wisdom from the Groundhog

Sensual Strings: The Art of Erotic Bondage

Whispered Flames: Unlocking the Power of Fire Play

Forgotten Shadows: A Guide to Cryptids Lost to Time

Six Weeks of Secrets: Groundhog Day's Hidden Messages

Shadows and Cycles: Groundhog Day Reflections

The Art of Love Letters: Crafting the Perfect Message

Romantic Getaways at Home: Turning Your Space into Paradise

Purrfect Brews: A Cat Lover's Guide to Coffee and Companionship

The Groundhog's Wisdom: Timeless Lessons for Modern Life

The Shadow Oracle: Groundhog Day as a Predictor

Emerging from the Burrow: A Journey of Renewal

The Language of Love: Learning Your Partner's Love Style

Authorpreneur: The Ultimate Blueprint for Writing, Publishing, and Thriving as an Author

Weathering the Seasons: Groundhog Day Perspectives

Valentine's Day Magic: A Guide to Romantic Rituals

The Shadow Chronicles: Stories of Groundhog Day

Love and Laughter: Fun Games for Valentine's Day

AstroRealty: Unlocking the Stars for Property Success

The Groundhog's Path: A Guide to Seasonal Balance

Groundhog Day Diaries: Reflections in the Shadow

The Groundhog's Light: Illuminating the Path Ahead

Valentine's Traditions from Around the World

AI Wealth Revolution: Unlocking the Trillionaire Mindset

Love Rekindled: Reigniting Passion in Relationships

Single and Thriving: Self-Love on Valentine's Day

Emerald Legends: Mystical Tales of Ireland

Green Alchemy: Harnessing Nature's Magic
The Hearts of Horror: A Valentine's Day Nightmare
The Leprechaun's Guide to Wealth and Wisdom
Dancing with the Sidhe: Celebrating the Otherworld
Shamrocks and Shadows: Mysteries of the Green Isle
Emerald Energy: Harnessing Luck and Growth
The Gingerbread Golem's Valentine: A Sweetheart's Guide to Love and Enchantment
The Celtic Knot: Weaving Life and Destiny
Green Fire: Elemental Magic for St. Patrick's Day
Clover Chronicles: Finding Your Inner Luck
Ireland's Mystical Creatures: A Field Guide
Gingerbread Golem's Love Almanac
Prowl and Thrive: The Lion's Guide to Success
Love Alchemy: Transforming Your Life Through Heart Energy
WORLD DOMINATION: Woman's Rule 3:The New Life
The Midnight Rose: A Guide to Lunar Love Spells
The Forbidden Letters: Writing Your Own Love Prophecy
Luck and Lore: St. Patrick's Day for Modern Mystics
The Green Path: A Pagan Celebration of Renewal
The Dark Architect's Guide to Reprogramming Reality
Prankster's Paradise: A Guide to Harmless Hijinks
Manifest Your Reality: The Law of Attraction Simplified
The TARDIS Owner's Manual: Understanding the Doctor's Ship: *A complete guide to the TARDIS, its technology, secrets, and mysteries*
Starlit Romance: Astrology Secrets for Finding True Love
The Time Lord's Atlas: A Complete Guide to the Whoniverse: ***A breakdown of the locations, planets, and dimensions explored in Doctor Who***
Sweetheart Shadows: The Dark Side of Love and Attraction
February Fire: Reigniting Passion in Every Area of Life

The Self-Love Toolkit: 5 Ways to Embrace Who You Are
February Sparks: Ignite Your Dreams in 28 Days
March to Success: A 31-Day Action Blueprint
Ancient Paths: The 13 Sacred Principles of Dino Wicca
Echoes of Tomorrow: Navigating the AI Revolution
The Wellness Blueprint: Balancing Mind, Body, and Soul
Green Horizons: Sustainable Living for a Better Tomorrow
The AI Wealth Code: How to Make Millions with Automation
AI-Powered Creativity: Writing, Art, and Music for Profit
Extinction Rites: Rebirthing Your Soul Through Prehistoric Magick
Sacred Serpents tarot
Celestial Enchantment blank journal
Star Strains
Culinary Journeys: Exploring Global Flavors at Home
The Hollowvale Curse
The Hollowvale Harvest
The Egg of Transformation: Awakening Your Inner Power
Blooming Into Power: A Wiccan Guide to Spring Awakening
The Nightmare Nexus: The Third Doctor's Perilous Haunting
Digital Detox: Reclaiming Your Life in a Connected World
Ostara's Path: Walking the Spiral of Renewal
The Sacred Hare
Financial Freedom: Building Wealth in the Modern Age
Spring's Cauldron: Stirring the Waters of Change
The Hollowvale Pact
Quantum Consciousness: The Science of Reality Shifting
The Hollowvale Hunger
The Sacred Waters Within: A Witch's Guide to Hydrocephalus Magick
The Raven's Nest: Building a Life of Unshakable Stability
AI and the Human Mind: The Future of Intelligence
The Hollowvale Reckoning

Timeless Love: Building and Maintaining Lasting Relationships

The Raven's Roar: Unlocking Unstoppable Confidence

Raven Sight: Awakening Intuition and Inner Wisdom

The Butterfly Effect: Small Changes, Big Transformations

Taming the Boogeyman: How to Conquer Your Inner Fears

The Magick of Green: Awakening Earth's Energy in You

The Entrepreneurial Mindset: Secrets to Business Success

The Hollowvale End

The Shadow Luck Ritual: Reclaiming Power from Your Dark Side

Spring Magick for Beginners: A Simple Guide to Seasonal Energy Work

Doctor Who: The Hollowvale Conundrum

The March of Miracles: Unlocking Synchronicities in Spring

Unveiling the Cosmos: A Guide to Stargazing and Space Exploration

The Ultimate Guide to Surviving an Economic Collapse

The AI Gold Rush: How to Profit from the AI Revolution

Bastet's Shadow: The Hidden Power of Feline Magick

The Bastet Codex: Unlocking the Goddess's Magickal Secrets

Purring Spells: Harnessing Bastet's Healing Frequencies

Bastet's Nine Lives: Rebirth, Transformation, and Immortality Spells

Primal Currents: Hydrocephalus Magick in the Path of Dino Wicca

The Digital Gold Rush: Mastering E-Commerce and Online Sales

Future Shock: Adapting to the Next Decade of Change

The Quantum Mindset: Think Like a Billionaire

Sacred Motherhood: Awakening the Divine Feminine Within

The Mother's Spellbook: Enchantments for Love, Protection, and Prosperity

The Witch's Guide to Parenting: Raising Empowered and Intuitive Children

The Magick of Motherhood: Reclaiming Your Power Through Rituals

The Pagan Path to Self-Love: A Goddess's Guide to Worth and Confidence

Wild Woman Magick: Unleashing Your Primal Power

The Money Magnet Blueprint: Unlocking Unlimited Wealth

Biohacking 101: Unlock Your Body's Full Potential

The Wild Father: A Pagan Guide to Strength and Wisdom

The Sacred Masculine: Unlocking Your Inner Power

The Druid's Compass

The Warrior's Mindset

The Father's Fire

Odin's Path

Ancestral Bonds

The House That Whispers

The Magician's Code

The Wild Hunt

The Green Man's Path

The Altar of Success

The Shadow and the Sword

The High Priestess's Guide to Energy Healing

The Lunar Mother

The Sacred Self-Care Grimoire

The Womb Wisdom Codex

The Wheel of the Mother

The Witch's Guide to Manifestation

The Q2 Reset

The Ultimate Guide to AI-Powered Passive Income

Escape the 9-5

AI Feline Fortunes

The Tear-Stained Grimoire

Razorblade Runes
Cemetery Sirens
The Midnight Wristwatch
The Town That Forgets
AI Horror & Creepypasta
The Hollow Frequency
The Breach Echo
The Quiet Between Worlds
The Sigil of Tharan-Khul
Summon the Vault of Y'ha'ten
The Becoming Codex
The Profit of Az'ra-nar
The Drowned Logos
Echoes of the Eldritch Will
The Deep Ledger
Necronomicon of Networth
Covenant of the Wealthwyrm
The Whisperer's Manifesto
The Rites of Azh-K'luth
The Ark of the Crawling Coin
The Tithe of Shadows
Inkheart Abyss
The Timewinds of Y'ha-nthlei
The Spiral Labyrinth of Azag-Nirrh
The Gallifreyan Heresy of the Black Pharaoh
The Psalms of Nyog-Sotha
Black Rain Alchemy
The Infinite Maw
The Entropic Blueprint
The Oracle of Sh'guul
The Book of Breach
The Drowned Saint's Testament
Dreamcraft of the Sleeper God

The Silence Market
Cthonomics: The Dark Wealth Algorithm
Invocation of the Ten-Eyed King
Wealthbound to the Wyrm Below
Become the Unnameable
Codex of the Sovereign Flame
Rituals of Relentless Becoming
The Shadow Ascends
The Eyes Beneath You
The Will That Wakes Worlds
Silence Is a Weapon
The Mirror That Screams
The Whisper Between Moments
The Mind That Devours Fear
The Myth of the Finished Self
The Architect of Your Madness
The Voice You've Buried
The Discipline of Madness
Stormborn: Awakening Your Inner Tempest
The Mind That Ate Time
Unbind Your Becoming
The Pact You Owe Yourself
The Devourer's Diet
The Acid That Carves the Path
The Tower You Must Burn
The Breath Between Worlds
Speak Like the Deep
The Labyrinth Within
The Spine of the Sea God
Rejection Is a Portal
The Crown You Refused
The Scar Is the Spell
The Lightless Flame

The Habit of Becoming Horrific
ChickenJockey Chaos
The Gatekeeper Within
You Are Not Your Name
The Compass of the Mad
The Archive of Unsent Letters
What the Mirror Can't Show You
The Knife You Needed
Worship Nothing, Become Everything
The Other Voice
The Body the World Forgot
The Vein of the Void
The Black Bone Codex
The Puzzle of the Hidden Self (Millennium Puzzle)
The Eye That Sees the Lie *(Millennium Eye)*
The Ring of Return (Millennium Ring)
The Rod of Relentless Will *(Millennium Rod)*
The Tally of the Soul (Millennium Tauk/Necklace)
The Key to the Locked Timeline (Millennium Key)
The Scale of Sacred Decisions (Millennium Scales)
Inferno Bites: The UnOfficial Minecraft Lava Cookbook
Rot in the Attic
Prana: The Hidden Force of Your Infinite Self
The Shadow Realm Within: Transforming Darkness Into Destiny
The Borderland Collapse
Claws of Protection: Bastet's Defensive Magick
Mr. Ring-a-Ding's Madness
Yugioh Astrology: Celestial Deckcraft and Duel Destiny (2026–2027 Edition)
The Seal You Signed: Unlocking the Power You Once Feared
The Puzzle of Infinite Minds: Unlocking the Mentalism Hidden Within

The Eye That Mirrors the All: Secrets of Inner Reflection
Doctor Who: The Toymaker's Broadcast
The Rod of Eternal Flow: Commanding the Currents of Vibration
Golden Eyes of Bastet: Enhancing Psychic Vision
The Key of Dual Forces: Balance Within the Polarity
The Scales of Living Rhythm: Timing the Dance of Life
The Necklace of Hidden Cause: Weaving the Webs of Fate
The Ring of Secret Masters: Rising Through the All Within All
Daggers of the Dying Deep
Bastet's Wealth and Fortune Magick: Prosperity Rituals of the Goddess
The Tide that Speaks
The Scrolls of Petosiris: 13 Rituals from the Feathered Eye
Petosiris and the Living Plague of Osirion
Feline Fire: Bastet's Passion and Love Magick
The Star Altar of Petosiris
Bastet's Whiskers: Supernatural Sensory Magick
The Bastet Grimoire
Feeding the Shadows
The Mouthless Prayer
The Spiral Wound
Becoming the Ibis: Lessons from Petosiris's Mind
The Crimson Coven: Cola Magick for Sweet Dominion
Sacred Cat's Paw
The Soda Zodiac: A Flavor for Every Sign
Covenant of the Crawling Flame
The Ink of Ish'Zur
Frothroot: The Thirst That Ate the World
The Golden Glyphs of Prosperity
The Etherbind Codex
Echoes of the Resistance: Reclaiming the You That Survived

Harnessed Minds: Breaking Free from Mental Control
The Eyes in the Smoke
Rootwake: The Carbon Covenant
Skitter Logic: Unlearning the Fear That Built You
Doctor Who: The World That Froths
Rootwake: The Fizz That Rewrites Flesh
Rootwake: Frothfather of the World
The Holly Pact: Blood Beneath the Mistletoe
The 2nd Mass Principle: Building Unbreakable Tribes
Web of Wits: A Survival Guide to Encounters with Anasi the Spider (Aunt Nancy)
The Hexbreaking Handbook: Effective Spells to Remove Curses
Pop Alchemy: Transform Your Life One Sip at a Time
The Mason Code: Leading in Unleadable Times
Petosiris and the Fifth Chamber of Thoth
The Ether Seed Within
The Parent of Tomorrow
Petosiris's Pyramid of Perpetual Wealth
Unlearn the World
Grimoire of the Hollow Tongue
Zodiac Weeds: Finding Your Strain Through the Stars
Aquarius Rises in the Bank
The Sugar God's Smile
The Skinclock Reversal: Biohacking the Face of Time
Debtburn: How to Obliterate What You Owe Forever
The Ice Cream Oracle: What Your Cone Says About Your Future
Silence Is Sovereignty: The Power of Being Unreadable
The Wind That Whispers Through Stone
Path of the Four Directions
Doctor Who: The Maestro's Symphony of Endings
Oxygen Grail: Breathing to Undo the Clock

Zodiacal Collapse: When Stars Devour Time

Teachings from the Red Sand Silence

Doctor Who: Omega – The Broken Equation

Memory Wipe Your Past: Start Over Like a MiB

Mitochondria Prime: Ignite the Core of Youth

A Nest of Roaches

Grub from the Galaxy: MiB Recipes You'll Never Forget

Whiskers of Power: Bastet's Guide to Inner Sovereignty

The Gift Must Cost Them: Negotiation Through Unequal Exchange

The Worm Guys' Wealth Code: Hustle Like an Alien

Bug Out: The Edgar Method for Ruthless Goal Setting

Weaving Life with Spiderwoman's Pattern

Doctor Who: The Rani's Renaissance

How to Get a Job (If You're a Puppygirl)

Speak Through Others: The Art of Proxy Power

T-Rex Your Trauma: Reclaim the Power of Your Primal Self

The Black Briefcase: How MiB Stay Wealthy in Silence

The Thirst Beyond Reason: Understanding Diabetes Insipidus From the Inside Out

Backwoods Witchcraft for Billionaires: The Pagan Path from Dirt Roads to Gold Roads

The Moonshine Grimoire: Fermented Spells for Abundance

The Nameless Geometry

The Wraith's Mixtape: Spellcasting with Songs of Sorrow

The Gallifreyan Gentleman: Silent Wealth, Sonic Confidence, and the Doctor's Code of Living

Sugar Water Confidence

Dino Totems: Spirit Guides from Earth's First Gods

Pumpkin Sigils & Ritual Smoke

The Hózhó Compass

The Distortus Discipline – Order from Inner Mutation

Witchcraft for the Cold-Blooded Soul

Moonlight Over the Blessingway

Water, Interrupted: When the Body Forgets How to Hold On

Deformed but Divine: Embracing Your Asymmetry

Hexes in the Henhouse: The Farm Witch's Guide to Power

The Reversed Flame: A Grimoire of Inverted Power

Salt, Cells, and Sanity: Reclaiming Balance with Diabetes Insipidus

King of the Broken: Crowning the Flawed Self

Moonlight Scars: Emo Moon Magick and the Art of Lunar Sorrow

Noose Spells: Magick of the Hanging Rope

The Goth Cathedral: Rituals of the Broken and Beautiful

The Cretaceous Codex: Dino Spirits and Fossil Magick

The Turkey Bones Ritual

Nine Lives of Manifestation: Unlocking Bastet's Reality Codes

Chaos Muscles: Building Strength from Twisted Pain

Emo Blood Magick: The Veins of Power

The 3AM Flood: Nighttime Urination, Sleep Loss, and the DI Spiral

The Silence Between the Stars

The Lemon Method: Sour Your Way to Success

Starlit Sovereign

The Rite of Twelve Gates: Walking the Gates of the Duat.

Cornbread and Conjure: Recipes for Riches and Rootwork

The Black Rose Rituals: Emo Love Spells and Obsession Magick

The Eternal Goodbye: Death Magick and Rebirth Rituals

Sinkrot: The Drain That Remembers

The Hybrid Mindset: Thinking Beyond Evolution

Bone Dry: Navigating Dehydration Before It Breaks You

Wreathcraft: Winter Sigils and Yuletide Spells

The Rite of Twelve Mouths

S'mores of the Damned: Haunted Recipes for Halloween Night

Rethink the Drink: A Beverage Survival Guide for DI Warriors

The Shadow Chord: Guitar Magick and Sonic

Malformed Yet Majestic: Leading When You Feel Wrong Inside

The Cursed Diary: Ink-Stained Spells of the Emo Soul

Anxiety Off Switch: Emergency Reset for a Fried Nervous System

The Energy Heist: How to Take Back Your Life from Drainers

Beyond the Bathroom: Rebuilding Your Social Life With DI

Coyote's Gift for Decision Makers

Ghoul-Goo: Spooky S'mores You'll Die For

Echoes in the Mirror: Scrying and Self-Destruction Magick

Thread and Thorn: Stitching Spells from Rural Cloth

The Mogwai Mind: Building Untouchable Wealth from Small Ideas

Be Your Own Guide: Trust Your Inner Compass

Hormones in Chaos: The Endocrine Puzzle of Diabetes Insipidus

ChronoCleanse: Detox Your Biological Timeline

The Limb You Hide Is the One That Saves You

Leaves, Bones, and Whisper Spells

The Dinosaur Mindset: Prehistoric Tactics for Modern Wealth

Clawing Back Control: A Bastet Method for Boundaries and Empowerment

Samhain Codes of the Forgotten

Orange Alchemy: The Autumnal Spellbook

Monster Within, Master Without

The Sigil That Sleeps

Hearthcraft: Yule Hearth Sigils and Winter Warmth Spells

Temple of the Purring Moon: Rituals from Bastet's Lineage
When the Earth Remembers Your Footsteps
Food for Mood: Eat to Heal Depression, Not Just Survive It
Witch of the Kudzu Vine: Southern Pagan Wealth Secrets
The Invisible Diagnosis: Advocating for Yourself With DI
The Coffin's Lullaby: Sleep Magick and Nightmares as Portals
Ashes of the Will: Rituals for Erasing the Self
The Fracture Rite: Shattering the Magickal Core
Funeral Candles: The Art of Emo Flame Magick
The Black Grimoire: A Blank Ritual for Writing in Absence
Phantom Thirst: A Halloween Survival Guide for Diabetes Insipidus
The Hollow Crown: Emo Royalty and Magick of the Outcast King
Sandpainting for the Soul
Falling Into Balance: Using the Extra Hour to Recalibrate Life
100 Southern Superstitions That Still Work
The DI Child: A Parent's Guide to Raising Hydrated, Happy Kids
The Jungle of Shame: Escaping the Hidden Lab of Doubt
The Witch's Toast: S'mores Spells and Creepy Confections
The Hoodoo Pantry: Spells from the Mason Jar
The Immortal Fortune: Secret Wealth Lessons from Captain Jack Harkness
The Specter's Embrace: Magick for Channeling Ghostly Lovers
Grateful Waters: A Thanksgiving Survival Guide for Diabetes Insipidus
The Seizure Gospel
Harvestbind: Autumn Sigils and Samhain Spells
Doctor Who: The Algorithmic Awakening
Silent Nights, Steady Waters: A Christmas Survival Guide for Diabetes Insipidus

The Extra Hour Effect: How One Hour Can Transform Everything

Blade Between the Breaths

Running with the Mountain Shadows

Echoes of the Failed Experiment – Becoming a Living Legacy

Swamp Witches & River Ghosts: Real Southern Hauntings

Cornbread Prophecies: Magical Recipes from a Southern Table

Doctor Who: The Signal in the Star

Bloomcraft: Spring Sigils and Equinox Enchantments

Vanisher: How to Disappear from the Internet Without Losing Your Life

The Ultimate Christmas Cookie Cookbook

The Unbreakable Parent: How to Mentally Survive Raising Kids in a Broken World

Time Debt: How to Reclaim the Hours You Didn't Know You Lost

One Month, One Million: Unconventional Cash Creation Tactics

Doctor Who: The Cyber Conversion Protocol

Black Friday Frenzy: The Art of Finding Hidden Online Deals

The Grimoire Buried Under the Apple Tree

Digital Couponing Masterclass: Your Step-by-Step Guide to Black Friday Savings

The Fire Inside the Flint

Shadows on the Ceiling: The Emo Guide to Astral Magick

The Bone-Eaters Beneath Us

Black Friday Bundle Blueprint: Creating Irresistible Product Packages for Maximum Sales

Thirteen Nights of Unbinding

Doctor Who: Engines of Influence

Pumpkin Spice Alchemy: Recipes of Fire and Frost

When Raptor Met Rexy: Prehistoric Lessons in Wild Romance
Oblivion's Candle: Burn the Path Behind You
Campfire Curses and Chocolate: A Halloween S'mores Grimoire
The Wallet That Wasn't Mine: Breaking Free from Inherited Scarcity
The Cola Zodiac: What Your Fizz Says About Your Fate
Frostfire Fortune: Unlocking Winter's Hidden Prosperity
Signal Jamming: Detox Your Brain from Info Overload
The Dust of the Forgotten Rite
The Golden Cat Sigils: Drawing Power in Bastet's Name
Mud Magick: The Prosperity of Getting Dirty
Savory Spicefall: Beyond the Pumpkin Pie
Pumpkin Spice Apothecary Kitchen
The Pumpkin Spice Economy: Turning Trends into Billions
The Ember Veil: 13 Nights of Fire Magick
Financial Freeze: When Earning Triggers Panic
The Gingerbread Alchemist: Sweet Recipes with a Twist
Biosynth Power: Programming Yourself from Scratch
Echoes from the Talking Circle
Truffle Alchemy: Fungus of Fortune
Spores of Power: The Truffle Witch's Handbook
Doctor Who: The Tower That Speaks
The Mycelium Veil: Truffle Magick Unbound
Broke But Ashamed: Healing the Shame Wound of Debt
The Evergreen Mind: Growth Through Winter Stillness
The Black Veil Truffle Rite
The Voice Beneath Symbols
Witchlight on the Bayou: Swamp Spells for Sovereignty
I Grew Up Poor and Now I Sabotage My Success
The Lantern of Hollow Souls

Get Some Tarot cards: https://www.makeplayingcards.com/sell/apophis-occult-shop

Get some shirts: https://www.bonfire.com/store/apophis-shirt-emporium/

Instagrams:
@apophis_enterprises,
@apophisbookemporium,
@apophisscardshop
Twitter: @apophisenterpr1
Tiktok:@apophisenterprise
Youtube: @sg1fan23477
Hive: @sg1fan23477
CheeLee: @SG1fan23477

Podcast: Apophis Chat Zone: https://open.spotify.com/show/5zXbrCLEV2xzCp8ybrfHsk?si=fb4d4fdbdce44dec

Newsletter: https://apophiss-newsletter-27c897.beehiiv.com/

If you want to support me or see posts of other projects that I have come over to: **buymeacoffee.com/mpetchinskg**

I post there daily several times a day

Get your Dinowicca or Christmas themed digital products, especially Santa Raptor songs and other musics. Here: **https://sg1fan23477.gumroad.com**

Apophis Yuletide Digital has not only digital Christmas items, but it will have all things with Dinowicca as well as other Digital products.

www.ingramcontent.com/pod-product-compliance
Lightning Source LLC
LaVergne TN
LVHW022228200926
848481LV00006B/2175
* 9 7 9 8 3 4 9 5 9 8 2 9 6 *